How to Pass

HIGHER
French
for CfE

Douglas Angus

HODDER
GIBSON
AN HACHETTE UK COMPANY

Audio files for the Listening tasks in this book are available online. Visit www.hoddergibson.co.uk and click on 'Updates and Extras'.

The Publishers would like to thank the following for permission to reproduce copyright material:

Acknowledgements

The reading passage "Le Français en vacances: ce qui a changé" (pp.3–4), questions (pp.4–7) and marking scheme (p.8); the personal response writing question (p.89); the contexts and topics grid in Appendix 1 (p.112); the talking and writing grammar guide in Appendix 2 (p.113); and the marking scheme tables in Appendices 3 and 4 (pp.114–119) copyright © Scottish Qualifications Authority.

The Directed Writing scenarios and questions (p.80) have been adapted from SQA past Higher paper: www.sqa.org.uk/files_ccc/ FrenchDirectedWritingSQPH.pdf copyright © Scottish Qualifications Authority.

The solutions to worked examples throughout the book are by the author.

The reading passage "La mode du sport : les baskets et les jogging !" (pp.20–21) is based on the article "Va y avoir du style" by Françoise-Marie Santucci, which appeared in *Liberation* on 16th June 2006, permission granted by EDD. Reading passage (pp.14–15) is adapted from "La vogue des rencontres sur Internet" published on DossierFamilial.com 5 September 2007; reading passage (pp.17–18) based on "Scolarité : le redoublement est-il un échec ?" also from DossierFamilial.com, published on 12 May 2014 ; reading passage (pp.23–24) is adapted from "SMS, textos : dites 'J't'M avec le pouce !" by Louis Asana published on Doctissimo.com.

Audio engineering: Phil Booth, Heriot-Watt University, Edinburgh.

Every effort has been made to trace all copyright holders, but if any have been inadvertently overlooked the Publishers will be pleased to make the necessary arrangements at the first opportunity.

Although every effort has been made to ensure that website addresses are correct at time of going to press, Hodder Gibson cannot be held responsible for the content of any website mentioned in this book. It is sometimes possible to find a relocated web page by typing in the address of the home page for a website in the URL window of your browser.

Hachette Livre UK's policy is to use papers that are natural, renewable and recyclable products and made from wood grown in sustainable forests. The logging and manufacturing processes are expected to conform to the environmental regulations of the country of origin.

Orders: please contact Bookpoint Ltd, 130 Park Drive, Abingdon, Oxon OX14 4SE. Telephone: (44) 01235 827720. Fax: (44) 01235 400454. Lines are open 9.00–5.00, Monday to Saturday, with a 24-hour message answering service. Visit our website at www. hoddereducation.co.uk. Hodder Gibson can be contacted direct on: Tel: 0141 848 1609; Fax: 0141 889 6315; email: hoddergibson@ hodder.co.uk

© Douglas Angus 2015

First published in 2015 by
Hodder Gibson, an imprint of Hodder Education,
An Hachette UK Company,
2a Christie Street
Paisley PA1 1NB

Impression number   5 4 3 2 1

Year   2019 2018 2017 2016 2015

Cover photo © Tiberius Gracchus – Fotolia
Illustrations by Barking Dog Art Design and Illustration
Typeset in India
Printed in Spain
A catalogue record for this title is available from the British Library.
ISBN: 978 1 471 83606 0

Contents

Introduction

This book is a guide to Higher French, to its four skill areas, and to how to get the best possible mark in each area. There are separate sections giving advice on reading, listening, talking and writing. For reading and listening, there are also practice questions, with answers so that you can check your work. For speaking and writing, we work through some sample questions, looking at how to improve your performance in assessments. Accompanying this book are soundfiles that can be downloaded from www.hoddergibson.co.uk (click on 'Updates and Extras'), and in the book there are questions and transcripts to go with these soundfiles.

What is involved in Higher French?

Higher French, like all your other Highers, and also like National 5, is a course that is tested by a mixture of internal (Unit) and external (Course) assessment. Both of these assess the four skills of reading, listening, talking and writing. There are two Units that make up your Higher: Understanding Language and Using Language. The Units are assessed by assessments chosen by your school or college. These could take a variety of forms, depending upon how your teacher decides to assess your work.

The Course is assessed in two ways. Firstly, you will have external exams in three of the skills: reading, writing and listening will be assessed at the end of the course in an external exam set and marked by SQA. What is new in Higher, as opposed to National 5, is translation: you will be asked to translate a short extract of the reading passage from French into English.

The assessment of talking is a bit different from the other areas: it will be assessed by a presentation and conversation with your teacher, which will be recorded. You can choose the subject of your talk and the following discussion. Your teacher will give you a grade for this, and this will be your final grade, subject to moderation by SQA. That means your teacher may be asked to send the recording off to SQA to be moderated. In nearly all cases, this means your teacher's mark will be your Higher mark. The good news is that talking at Higher follows exactly the same rules as talking at National 5, with just a change to the length of time you are expected to talk, so you should know exactly what you are doing here!

How is my final mark made up?

This is very straightforward, as all your marks for the various parts of the exam are added together to make up your final mark. Your marks will also be your percentages. This means you can fail an individual part of the exam, but still pass overall. Normally, 70 per cent is an A, 60 per cent is a B, 50 per cent a C and 45 per cent will get a D.

Talking

This is marked out of 30, so that is 30 per cent of your mark. Ten marks are for the presentation, 15 for the conversation, and 5 are for 'sustaining performance'. You can find more about this in the chapter on talking (Chapter 9).

Reading and translation

This makes up 30 per cent of your mark. Twenty marks are for the answers to the questions on the passage, 10 for the translation.

Directed writing

You will be asked to write an account, in French, of a visit you have made to, or an experience you have had in, a French-speaking country. (You do not actually have to have made this visit: it can be imaginary.) There will be a choice of two topics, taken from two of the four contexts of Society, Learning, Employability and Culture. You will be asked to address four specific bullet points. This will be worth 10 marks.

Listening

This is worth 20 marks. You will hear a presentation or monologue, followed by a dialogue. The topic will be taken from one of the four contexts of Society, Learning, Employability and Culture.

Personal response writing

You will also have to write your own opinions on the topic of the Listening exam in French. Normally you will be asked to respond to three questions. This writing will be worth 10 marks.

What do I have to know?

You will be expected to know all the basic vocabulary of French, but also vocabulary covering a list of the contexts and topic areas of Higher, which are in the structures and vocabulary chapter (Chapter 12). This will help you listen to and read French more easily. In this book we have reprinted basic vocabulary to help you revise, and have added to this useful vocabulary for each of the four contexts of Higher.

You will also need to know more about grammar than you did at National 5, so that you can write and speak French at the appropriate level for Higher. Your writing should show you have some knowledge of grammar, and you must work at getting your structures and endings right. The grammar guide in the chapter on structures and vocabulary (Chapter 12) should give you an idea of what you are expected to know. In talking, your teacher and examiner will be looking for you to demonstrate a knowledge of structure, verbs and the other aspects of language that are in the grammar guide.

You must also be able to use a good dictionary to help you understand French in the Reading and Listening exams, and to let you find words you need for your talking and writing. This means you need to know properly how your dictionary works, how to look up things quickly and how to interpret what you find when you have looked something up. You will find some advice on this in the reading chapter of this book (Chapter 1).

What exactly is involved in the exam?

There are two parts to the exam: the first part will often take place in February or March, and will be your Talking assessment. The second part is Papers 1, 2 and 3, which you will sit in May. Paper 1 lasts an hour, and is made up of Reading and Translation. Paper 2, Directed Writing, lasts for forty minutes. Paper 3 is Listening and Personal Response (opinion) Writing, and will last for one hour.

Talking

Talking will be assessed by your teacher and externally moderated by SQA, as we have already seen. What you talk about should be organised between you and your teacher.

You will have to carry out two tasks:
- A presentation to your teacher on a topic you choose (using no more than five headings of up to eight words each in English or in French). This should last about two minutes.
- A conversation with your teacher, starting on the same topic. This should last about five minutes. You must move on to another topic area during the course of the conversation.

While the presentation is something you have absolute control over, you must be ready to carry on the conversation into other areas that will develop from the initial part of the conversation. However, remember it is a conversation, and you also can lead it where you want it to go. We will give you some advice on this in the chapter on talking (Chapter 9).

Listening

For the Course, listening will be assessed by the external Higher examination. This will be a recording of a monologue by one French speaker, followed by a dialogue between two French speakers, and you will be asked to give answers based upon what you hear. The monologue will last up to two minutes, and the dialogue will last over two minutes. You will hear them both twice (not three times as at National 5 level). There will be a gap between the monologue and the dialogue, and you will be warned when there is a minute to go till the start of the dialogue.

The questions will be set and answered in English, and will follow the order of the dialogue. You will be allowed to use a French–English dictionary, and we will give you advice on this in the chapter on listening (Chapter 5).

Reading and translation

The Course Reading paper is one longer text, of about 600 words, with questions that will be set and answered in English. You may well find unusual words translated for you in a glossary. You will be allowed to use a French dictionary, and will have to be good at using this, as otherwise you will spend so much time looking up words, you will never finish answering the questions!

One part of the reading text will be underlined (usually a small paragraph, or three to four sentences) and you will be asked to translate this into English.

Most of the questions will follow the order of the text, and you will be guided as to where to find the answers. However, one question will ask you to identify the overall purpose or meaning of the text.

Writing

Writing will be assessed in two ways. You will have to produce two pieces of writing in your final exam:

- **Directed writing** of 120 to 150 words, which will be an account of a journey or experience you have made, chosen from two options. There will be four bullet points to address, which you should attempt to answer at roughly equal length.
- **Personal response writing**, also of 120 to 150 words, which will be linked to the topic discussed in the listening. There will be three questions as part of the task to address, which you should again attempt to answer at roughly equal length.

For both of these pieces of writing you will be allowed a dictionary.

What grammar do I need to know?

When marking your work, teachers will be looking for a variety of different structures, a good level of accuracy in basic structures and some control of more complex language. You will be allowed to make some errors, but this will affect the grade you are awarded. You should be able to show you can do everything listed in the box on page viii.

For better grades, you will have to do more than this. Marking schemes show what markers are going to be looking for, and the marking schemes and grade descriptors for Writing and Talking, which you will find in Appendix 3 and Appendix 4, will give you a clear idea of what you should be able to do to achieve a good mark.

What you should know

Verbs

★ Use the correct form of the present, imperfect, perfect, future and conditional tenses, and use modal verbs correctly.
★ Use *ne … pas, ne … jamais*, and so on.
★ Use relative pronouns and conjunctions.
★ Know the irregular verbs.

Nouns and pronouns

★ Use the correct type of article/determiner (a, the, this), and the correct form (e.g. correct gender or number).
★ Use the correct pronouns, and put them in the right place.
★ Use the correct plural forms.

How do I go about learning vocabulary?

The best way to revise is to practise. Although different people have different ways of learning vocabulary, the following ways might be useful to you:

Hints & tips

✓ Try writing down a list of words, then reading them out. Cover up the French, and see if you can remember it from the English, and of course the other way round.
✓ Read vocabulary/texts over several times, on different occasions.
✓ Check your memorising, by either covering one part and remembering the other, or by getting someone (a friend or a parent) to do it with you. If you have someone who will help you, get them to say a word in English, which you have to put into French.
✓ Try to get your words organised into areas, so they all hang together and make sense to you.
✓ Use spidergrams of related words.

Appendix 1 gives an overview of all the topic areas that might come up, and in Chapter 12 you will find both basic vocabulary and vocabulary that you might come across in each of the four contexts of Society, Learning, Employability and Culture.

Reading

Introduction

Answering the questions in your Reading paper is worth **20 per cent** of your final mark in Higher French; you will also have to translate a short passage from the text you read into English, for a further **10 per cent**. You will have about one hour to read the text, answer the questions and do the translation. The text will be about 600 words long. You will be able to use a dictionary for this exam, and so you need to be very confident in your dictionary use. As part of your Understanding Language Unit assessment, before you sit the final exam, you will also have to demonstrate your ability in reading. However, the format of this will be up to your teacher or school to decide.

When you sit the exam, you will have one hour for the paper which has reading and translation. It is up to you how to divide the time, and what order to do the paper in, but as a rough guideline you should spend around 50 minutes on the reading and about ten minutes on the translation. You can start off with either the reading or directed writing paper. Some people prefer to start off with the translation, to 'get it out the way', but it is a much better plan to leave the translation till after you have finished the questions, as you are likely to have a deeper understanding of the text by then, and will find that a help with the translation. The translation is a short passage, broken into five chunks for marking, and you will get a mark out of 2 for each chunk.

Just as at National 5, you do not have to understand all of the text thoroughly for most of the questions: you have to get the gist of the text, and then identify carefully the location of the answers you need, taking more time with these areas of the text. The final question, worth 2 marks, will require you to have an overall understanding of what the text is about, but again you do not have to understand every word to have a feeling for the overall meaning.

Reading is a skill, and a skill you need to work on to allow you to give of your best in the final exam. You are not expected to give every detail, or translate word for word what is in the French text. Sometimes the details will matter, but what is more important is that you demonstrate you have understood what the text is about, and put your answers into good English. If your answers do not make sense, then you can assume they are wrong! You do not have to answer in sentences, but be careful not to give answers that are too short.

⇨

Ses vêtements se sont féminisés. Elle se promène avec un sac
40 en paille sur l'épaule et, sur le nez, elle a posé des lunettes avec
montures interchangeables qu'elle peut assortir à son T-shirt.

Son compagnon est lui aussi devenu plus sobre. Maintenant, il
porte des vêtements en fibres naturelles, et il aime le style sportif
américain, avec des T-shirts XXL, extra-extra larges, qui laissent
45 une impression de liberté. Seule fantaisie: un bandana corsaire
sur la tête. S'il porte des lunettes, elles sont rondes à la Lennon,
noires ou en écaille. Mais surtout pas (quelle horreur!) colorées.

La façon de se bronzer a changé

Et puis, si on veut vraiment bronzer, il faut le faire intelligemment,
en bougeant et non pas bêtement étendu sur son drap de bain.
50 Toujours très en vogue: le frisbee et le badminton. Tout nouveau,
en revanche: le scatch, un jeu tout simple qui consiste à envoyer
une balle que le partenaire rattrape avec un petit disque couvert
de Velcro.

Pourquoi le vacancier français a-t-il fait tous ces changements?
55 Alors il y a un peu de tout. L'amour de son pays, le désir d'être
plus écologiste, la recherche d'un nouvel art de vivre.

Glossary

se ruer (dans): *to dash (into)*

un hors-bord: *speedboat*

Question ?

Re-read lines 8–21.

1 French people have changed where they choose to go.
   a) In what way has their choice of destination changed? Give details. **2**

   ....

   ....

*You are asked to give details about how things have changed: there are
two marks, so go for before and after: you are told where to look, and you
can then find in the passage that* le vacancier ne se lance plus: *subject and
verb mean the holidaymaker no longer dashes: (watch that reflexive verb!)
towards the south, sun and heat. The passage then goes on* Il cherche, *that
is, he looks for...*

Question ?

b) What do many people now prefer? State three things. **3**

....

....

....

The question says 'State three things', so after 'prefer' you should find three things to mention. The magic word to look for is préfèrent, *as this is the value judgement.*

Question ?

c) Why has Brittany become even more popular? **1**

....

You can find popularité *and* la Bretagne *easily. A little trick here:* D'où *means 'that is why', so the answer is just before this.*

Question ?

Re-read lines 22–32.

2   Holiday activities have also changed.
a) Which kinds of activities are no longer popular? Give details. **1**

....

One mark, but the question asks for 'activities' in the plural, so mention them all! If in doubt when answering a question, give details, as long as you are sure they are correct.

Question ?

b) What do holidaymakers now prefer to do? State any **one** thing. **1**

....

This means there is more than one answer, so choose the one you find easier, and move on to the next question; you don't need to find more than one answer.

Notice if you miss out 'young', you lose both marks. Making a mistake between singular and plural also loses you both marks. The translation here should be more or less word for word. However, the last sense unit is different:

Text	Good 2	Satisfactory 1
qui a pour but d'attirer notre compassion. qui a pour but d'attirer notre compassion.	with the aim of attracting our compassion. that/which aims to whose aim/goal is to which is aimed at the purpose/intention of which is with the aim/objective of (to) attract/(of) attracting (to) arouse/engage our compassion/sympathy/pity	to/in order to (to) entice (to) lure (to) incite (to) gain/win (to) appeal to (to) draw your

The French literally says 'which has for goal to attract our compassion', which of course makes no sense in English, so we have to change it around to make sense in English. Getting right what you should leave and what you should change is the hardest part of doing a translation. Practice will make you better at this. Try to translate the rest of the extract:

> des centaines de « Mendiants d'Internet » ont créé des sites simplement pour faire appel à la générosité des autres. Chacun a une histoire à raconter

Note that *mendiant* means 'beggar'. The suggested answer is at the end of this chapter.

Guidance

The rules for understanding the French in order to make a translation are the same as for answering questions: look for the verbs first, find the subjects of these verbs and the rest should fall into place more easily. There are some differences here, however. You need to give **all** the details; you must answer in sentences if the original is in sentences; and you have to get details just right. It is no good getting the right verb, for instance, but the wrong tense.

There are some important points to remember.

Remember

☞ If what you have written does not make sense in English, then it is guaranteed to be wrong.

⇨

⇒
☞ Make sure you use the correct tense of the verb.
☞ Do not miss out any adjectives or adverbs: it is easy to forget a little word, and most marks are lost this way.
☞ Missing out one word can lose you both marks for that sense unit: check afterwards that you have included everything, perhaps by striking out the words on the question paper.
☞ You do not have to do a word-for-word translation, but just translate the sense of the original into English with all the details in place.

Try translating small chunks of text from any passage you read to get into the habit of translating, and discuss your answers with others. Another useful task is to take a piece of French text and run it through a translation machine or site on the internet such as Babelfish or Google Language tools. This will give you a translation that will probably be in bad English, and will not always make sense. Try to make it make sense in English, looking at the original and coming up with a proper translation. This will develop your attention to detail, and help you think about the quality of the English in your answer. And remember, if you put your own English text into a translation machine, and ask it to translate it into French, the result will probably be in bad French and not always make sense!

Sample paper translation

Comme l'année dernière et les années précédentes,

Like last year and the years before,

il a réservé des chambres dans un bel hôtel pas trop loin de la plage.

he reserved rooms in a nice hotel not too far from the beach.

Les enfants vont jouer dans la mer

The children go and play in the sea

pendant que maman passe la journée à se bronzer

while mum spends the day getting a tan/sunbathing

et que papa boit du vin avec le voisin.

and dad drinks wine with the neighbour.

Past paper translation

Encouraged by the success of this girl from New York, hundreds of 'Internet Beggars' have created sites simply to appeal to the generosity of others/other people. Each one has a story to tell with the aim of attracting our compassion.

Questions ?

This article describes how French people use the internet to find partners.

Re-read lines 4–9.

1 Patricia has started to use the internet to meet people.
 a) When exactly does she do this? Give details. **3**

 ....

 ....

 ....

 b) Who does she chat to? **1**

 ....

Re-read lines 10–23.

2 We learn why people go on to the chat sites.
 a) Can you give any two reasons? **2**

 ....

 ....

 b) What do the chat sites hope to do? **2**

 ....

 ....

 c) Why have so many people started to go on to this kind of site? **2**

 ....

 ....

Re-read lines 24–30.

3 The author suggests this may just be for very fashionable people.
 a) Does he agree? Give a reason for your answer. **1**

 ....

 b) What were the usual ways of meeting people previously? **2**

 ....

 ....

Re-read lines 35–45.

4 Patricia explains how she got started with online chatting.
 a) In what way did she first hear about it? **1**

 ....

 b) What is Patricia looking for? **1**

 ....

Re-read lines 46–51.

5 We learn how to sign up for one of these sites.
 a) What should we choose? **1**

 ....

 b) What two things should we not use? **2**

 ....

 ....

⇨

⇨

6 Now consider the article as a whole. Does the author give the impression that using meeting sites is a positive step? Give details from the text to justify your answer. **2**

....

....

Total **20**

7 Now translate lines 31–34 (Je … nouveaux.).

Example 2

This article discusses the system in France where children are often asked to repeat a year.

Scolarité : le redoublement est-il un échec ?

Des études statistiques menées en France ont montré qu'en moyenne, chaque année, plus de 60 000 élèves sont victimes de redoublement. Le redoublement scolaire est-il nécessaire ou non ? Voilà la question fondamentale que se posent les parents et les
5 enseignants d'aujourd'hui. Suites à des études statistiques, sur un échantillon de 1000 individus, dont parents et enseignants, 65 % des parents et 58 % des enseignants enquêtés déclarent être pour le redoublement des élèves. Ainsi, selon ces derniers, c'est le meilleur moyen pour aider les enfants en difficulté. Toutefois, pour
10 certains, redoubler est une perte de temps. En effet, il constitue plutôt une sorte de démotivation pour les élèves qu'une aide. Des études comparatives entre plusieurs pays ont montré que les pays qui affichent un taux de redoublement élevé sont beaucoup moins performants, sur le plan éducatif, que ceux dont le taux est faible.

15 Dans quelle mesure un redoublement peut-il être positif ? <u>Le redoublement peut être une chance pour l'élève qui a connu un drame dans sa vie (une mort dans la famille, par exemple) et pour celui qui a un niveau scolaire un peu juste mais fait néanmoins des efforts pour avoir de meilleurs résultats.</u> Valérie Sultan, professeur

⇨

20 principal en classe de troisième, raconte qu'un redoublement n'est
pas forcément synonyme d'échec. Au contraire, il peut permettre
à l'enfant de repartir sur des bases nouvelles. Mais faire redoubler
un élève, c'est toujours un pari. Elle parle aussi par exemple
d'un enfant de sixième qui éprouve des difficultés à s'adapter
25 à l'enseignement du collège, ou à un adolescent qui, en pleine
transformation physique et psychologique, est préoccupé par autre
chose que l'école et a besoin de respirer quelques mois. Mais il est
important de se souvenir du fait que, pour que le redoublement
soit une chance, il ne faut pas le présenter comme une punition.

30 Faut-il **faire le forcing*** pour faire passer son enfant dans
la classe supérieure ? Il est toujours préférable de discuter
d'abord avec l'école. Conseillers d'orientation et professeurs
travaillent tous dans l'intérêt de l'élève. Lorsqu'on est parent, on
a une relation intime avec son enfant. Du coup, on ne voit pas
35 forcément la réalité, et on peut se tromper. Les enseignants peuvent
avoir davantage de distance. Valérie Sultan raconte que, lors des
rencontres parents–professeurs, les profs sont ainsi capables de
repérer que le désir de l'un n'est pas forcément celui de l'autre : par
exemple, les parents veulent absolument que leur enfant fasse une
40 seconde générale avec l'intention de préparer le bac scientifique,
alors que l'élève a un autre projet en tête.

Valérie Sultan pense qu'il y a des classes où il est préférable de ne
pas contester le redoublement. Ce sont les classes « importantes » :
la sixième et la quatrième, au cours de laquelle les élèves
45 apprennent une seconde langue vivante. Quant à la troisième,
après avoir évalué le niveau des élèves à la fin de leur temps en
collège, les écoles ne retiennent le redoublement que pour une
petite partie d'entre eux. On propose que les autres adolescents en
difficulté sont orientés vers un lycée professionnel. Dans les classes
50 de sixième, quatrième et troisième, ce sont tous les professeurs de
la classe qui décident de faire passer ou redoubler l'enfant. Si la
famille veut contester son choix, elle est obligée de faire appel. En
cinquième, c'est différent : les professeurs donnent des conseils sur
l'orientation. C'est la famille qui prend la décision finale.

Glossary

faire le forcing   *put on pressure*

Questions ❓

Re-read lines 1–14.

1 The article starts with an overview of the system.
   a) What statistics does the article give about repeating a year in France? **3**

   ....

   ....

   ....

⇨

b) What negative effect might repeating a year have on children? **1**

....

c) What do comparative studies in different countries show? **1**

....

Re-read lines 19–29.

2 Mme Sultan talks about in what way repeating a year can be positive.
   a) Why might it be a good chance for a pupil? **1**

....

   b) She mentions two further cases where it could be advisable. Give details. **2**

....

....

   c) What is it important to bear in mind? **1**

....

Re-read lines 30–41.

3 We learn about the danger of putting too much pressure on the pupil.
   a) What should parents do? **1**

....

   b) Why should they do this? **2**

....

....

   c) When does Mme Sultan notice that parents do not always see things correctly? **1**

....

   d) What do teachers often notice? **2**

....

....

Re-read lines 42–54.

4 In some classes parents should just accept that their child should repeat the year, according
   to Mme Sultan.
   a) Why do very few pupils repeat troisième (fourth year)? **2**

....

....

   b) What is different about the situation in cinquième (second year)? **1**

....

5 Now consider the article as a whole. Do the authors give the impression that they are in
   favour of repeating, against it, or trying to give a balanced view? Give details from the text
   to justify your answer. **2**

....

....

Total **20**

6 Now translate lines 15–19 (Le … résultats.).

Example 3

This article discusses the pressures fashion puts on people.

La mode du sport : les baskets et les jogging !

On est en 1986. Les dirigeants de la marque aux trois bandes signent avec Run DMC le premier contrat non-sportif de l'histoire du marchand du sport : un million de dollars. Dans un seul week-end, il se vend pour 22 millions de dollars de produits siglés
5 Adidas–Run DMC. Aujourd'hui, 79 % des jeunes Français de 8 à 19 ans, quand ils pensent à des marques de vêtements, citent des griffes de sport. Stella McCartney **fait un malheur*** chez Adidas depuis qu'elle y dessine une collection. Une génération d'urbains adeptes du « cool » se retrouve dans les modèles de Puma, qui
10 collabore avec Philippe Starck ou Alexander McQueen.

Les trois grandes marques Nike, Adidas et Puma sont en train de quitter le sport pour la mode. <u>Jusqu'à présent, pour les marques de sport, toute leur énergie était consacrée à la technologie et la performance. Les femmes, qui ne représentent que 30 % de la</u>
15 <u>clientèle, constituent « le » marché de demain. Avant, on prenait les vêtements pour hommes, on les taillait plus courts et plus étroits et voilà, c'était la ligne féminine.</u>

Un responsable du style chez Nike à Portland (Oregon, États-Unis) peut-il séduire une consommatrice parisienne devouée à la mode ?
20 Pas vraiment. Les Américains pensent encore que les filles, c'est du rose et blanc porté assez large, quand les Londoniennes ou Parisiennes ont adopté jeans serré et look rock. Les dirigeants de Nike ont pris en compte l'existence du consommateur mode. Conséquence : on a recruté en Europe des dénicheurs de
25 tendances dont la mission est d'envoyer à Portland des comptes rendus réguliers sur l'évolution des modes dans la rue.

⇨

⇨

On va s'orienter vers la mode, oui, et vers les femmes, c'est certain, mais avec des stylistes maison. Après tout, l'entreprise au swoosh est l'une des plus grandes employeuses de designers au monde.

30 Contrairement aux Allemandes (des sportives sérieuses) ou aux Britanniques (des fanatiques de running), les Françaises sont avant tout folles de style. À elles les collections de Stella McCartney, petits **hauts*** couleur taupe et bas de jogging serrés. Les gens d'Adidas ont fait le même calcul que ceux de Nike : les
35 femmes ! Et pour les conquérir il faut insister sur le côté mode et style, à la différence des acheteurs hommes, qui sont encore centrés sur le sport.

La collaboration de Stella McCartney avec la marque est née un jour de 2000 lors d'une table ronde réunissant, autour des
40 collaborateurs d'Adidas, des créateurs venus parler style. Et Stella, qui est une sportive (natation, yoga), a pu dire : « Pourquoi est-on obligées de ressembler à des sacs ? » Depuis, elle et ses collaborateurs londoniens travaillent avec le bureau de style d'Adidas, en Allemagne.

45 Quant à Puma, quoi alors ? Voilà la description de l'acheteur type Puma : « Ce n'est pas forcément le mec le plus beau, le meilleur, mais c'est le plus cool, et sa copine est la mieux. » Car, avec des bureaux de style à Londres, Boston et à Herzogenaurach, plus de 100 personnes en tout, sans compter une cellule « sport fashion »
50 d'une cinquantaine de designers à Londres, Puma se trouve branché. « Les coupes sont près du corps, les matières légères, les shorts descendent aux genoux, même nos étiquettes sont rigolotes. »

Qui inventera l'équivalent du sweat à capuche du XXIe siècle ?
55 Une chose est certaine : les marques de sport font la jonction entre les différents styles et looks de la rue. Le vintage, toujours ; les sports « *porteurs d'image* » (surf, skate) bien sûr ; et les collections femmes, évidemment. Dans le textile, les hauts se vendent mieux que les bas, car le jeans joue désormais le rôle du casual. Le
60 jackpot reviendra à la marque qui inventera de quoi habiller les femmes en bas. Trois, deux, un, partez !

Glossary

| faire un malheur | *be a smash hit, great success* |
| un haut | *a top (article of clothing)* |

Questions ?

This article describes how important fashion is to sports clothes in France.

Re-read lines 1–10.

1   We read some background information.
   a) Why are the rap group Run DMC mentioned? **2**

   ....

   ....

   b) What statistic do we learn about young French people? **1**

   ....

Re-read lines 18–28.

2   We read how Nike is dealing with the issue.
   a) How do young Americans and young French girls differ in their approach to fashion? **2**

   ....

   ....

   b) What are Nike doing about this? **2**

   ....

   ....

Re-read lines 30–44.

3   The author talks about Adidas.
   a) What Adidas products do young French girls like? **2**

   ....

   ....

   b) What differences between male and female customers are noticed? **2**

   ....

   ....

   c) The article describes how Stella McCartney came to work with Adidas. Give two details of this. **2**

   ....

   ....

Re-read lines 45–53.

4   We learn about Puma's involvement in sports fashion.
   What description does Puma give of their average male customer? **3**

   ....

   ....

   ....

Re-read lines 54–59.

5   The author looks to the future.
   a) What question does the author ask? **1**

   ....

   b) Why do sports tops sell better than sports trousers? **1**

   ....

   ⇒

6 Now consider the article as a whole. Does the author give the impression that he is in favour of or against sporting fashion? Give details from the text to justify your answer. **2**

....

....

Total **20**

7 Now translate lines 12–17 (Jusqu'à présent ... la ligne féminine.).

Example 4

You come across this article about texting.

SMS, textos : dites « Je t'M » avec le pouce !

En quelques années, les mini-messages ou SMS ont conquis tous les propriétaires de mobile ! À tel point que le pouce est devenu un organe de communication à part entière. Qui aujourd'hui envoie
5 encore une lettre d'amour par la poste pour la Saint-Valentin ? Un message texte suffit !

Plus de quatre-vingt-douze pour cent des gens possèdent un téléphone portable en Europe. Et les SMS sont devenus une partie essentielle de cette révolution numérique. En Angleterre, plus d'un milliard de messages sont envoyés par mois. En France, ce sont
10 35 millions de vœux électroniques qui ont été échangés le premier janvier 2013.

Qui sont les « texters » ?

Mais qui sont les agités du pouce ? Si tout le monde envoie des messages de temps en temps, les véritables adeptes, qui privilégient ce moyen de communication, sont essentiellement les plus jeunes.
15 90 % des ados préféreraient envoyer des messages que de parler de vive voix au téléphone. Et les jeunes adultes ne sont pas en reste : 78 % des Français de 18–24 ans sont des habitués des SMS. Les

⇨

femmes seraient un peu plus textos que les hommes, mais on ne peut guère parler de la féminisation du pouce : les hommes s'en
20 servent chaque jour aussi ! Les utilisations majoritaires seraient les messages d'amour, l'amitié et autres fonctions plutôt relationnelles et sociales. Le développement des textos est tel que certains spécialistes n'hésitent pas à parler d'addiction, et des cliniques proposent même des cures de désintoxication.

Un monde à part

25 Mais surtout aujourd'hui les messages textes sont devenus un moyen à part entière de contacter son réseau de proches. Et cela s'adresse pratiquement exclusivement au cercle d'amis : une étude anglaise a montré que les « texters » n'envoient pas des SMS indifféremment à tout leur carnet d'adresse. Ils envoient de
30 manière intensive des textos à un petit groupe d'amis. Les SMS sont envoyés moins facilement à un membre de la famille.

À noter que de nouvelles fonctionnalités, telles que l'accès aux logiciels de messagerie instantanée du web sur son mobile, devraient renforcer ce phénomène.

Le pouce des timides

35 Certains spécialistes pensent que les textos sont, encore plus que les forums de discussions, la bouée de sauvetage des grands timides et les phobiques sociaux. En clair, tous ceux qui ont du mal à s'exprimer en face à face. Ces véritables « handicapés sociaux » en sont réduits à même éviter la conversation
40 téléphonique pour lui préférer le message texte. Des scientifiques ont montré que les personnes qui ont tendance à nouer des amitiés plutôt dans le monde virtuel de l'Internet sont aussi plus attirées par les messages textes. Les SMS seraient même utilisés par certains à la manière d'un « chat ». Avec l'avantage pour les
45 timides d'avoir plus de temps pour réfléchir à ses réponses.

Y a klk1 ?

Si le SMS est devenu un mode de communication à part entière, il a aussi son langage ... qui d'ailleurs **hérisse le poil*** des puristes. Écriture phonétique, lettres qui remplacent des syllabes ... Pour les plus âgés, cela ne ressemble à rien. Celui-ci renforce encore plus
50 le sentiment d'appartenance à un groupe, avec son langage et ses codes. Mais ses détracteurs soulignent que cette simplification limite la richesse de la discussion. Il est difficile en effet de philosopher en langage SMS ... On notera néanmoins des initiatives intéressantes, telles que les fables de La Fontaine en SMS publiées par Phil Marso.

55 Même si vous êtes un adepte des SMS, n'oubliez pas tout de même de rencontrer vos amis dans la vraie vie. Et alors éteignez votre portable !

Glossary

hérisser le poil   *annoy*

Questions ❓

This article describes how texting is becoming more used in France.

Re-read lines 6–11.

1 The article gives some information about the growth of texting in Europe. What three statistics does it state? **3**

....

....

....

Re-read lines 12–22.

2 The article goes on to discuss who is using texting.
   a) Which group of people use texts most? **1**

   ....

   b) What do we learn about the relative use by men and women? **1**

   ....

   c) What are the main reasons for using texts? **2**

   ....

   ....

Re-read lines 25–34.

3 The author talks about who is texted.
   a) Who are the main recipients of text messages? **1**

   ....

   b) Who is less likely to receive a text? **1**

   ....

   c) What is likely to increase text use in the future? **1**

   ....

Re-read lines 35–45.

4 We learn more about texters.
   a) Who is texting really useful for? **1**

   ....

   b) Why is this the case? State two reasons. **2**

   ....

   ....

⇨

⇨
  b) Teachers advise, but familes make the
     final decision **1**
5 They are trying to give a balanced view:
   often the author asks questions, and gives
   two different viewpoints/They quote Mme
   Sultan who is in favour/but refer to pupils as
   'victims'/Some people say it is the best thing,
   others say it is a waste of time/They quote
   statistics saying most people are in favour, but
   balance that with statistics to show it might
   not be effective/When they talk about not

disagreeing with repeating, they make it clear
they are quoting a point of view/They never
give an opinion of their own **2**

Total **20**

6 Repeating can be an opportunity for a pupil/
   who has experienced a drama in his or her
   life/(a death in the family, for instance)/and
   for the one who is not doing very well in
   school/but nevertheless is making efforts to
   get better marks.

Answers

La mode du sport : les baskets et les jogging !

1 a) They signed the first non-sporting
      contract/with Adidas (the sports goods
      manufacturer)/They sold 22 million dollars'
      worth of Adidas products the first weekend
      they were on sale
      (Any two) **2**
   b) 79% mention sports clothing names
      when they are thinking about brands **1**
2 a) Young American girls are supposed
      to wear pink and white sports clothing,
      worn loose/Young French girls
      (Parisian girls) like tight jeans and rock
      clothes **2**
   b) They have recruited people to research
      street trends in Europe/and send the results
      to HQ/Portland **2**
3 a) Taupe-coloured tops/Tight-fitting
      leggings **2**
   b) Males are more focused on sport/Female
      customers on fashion and style **2**
   c) It started at a round table discussion in
      2000/for Adidas and creators to discuss

style/Stella was into sport and asked why
sports clothing looked awful
(Any two) **2**

4 He may not be the best-looking guy/but he is
   the coolest/and his girlfriend is the best **3**
5 a) Who will invent the equivalent of the
      hoodie for the 21st century? **1**
   b) Jeans are still seen as casual wear **1**
6 The author is in favour of this style of fashion:
   he uses words like *cool* and *branché* (up-to-
   date) very often/He cites names from fashion
   and music/He discusses how successful Stella
   McCartney has been/He gives positive reports
   about what Adidas and Puma are doing/In
   the last paragraph he looks forward to the
   future **2**

Total **20**

7 Until now, for sports brands,/all their energy
   was concentrated on technology and
   performance./Women, who only represent
   30% of their customers, make up *the* market of
   tomorrow./Before, they took men's clothes, cut
   them shorter and narrower,/and there you had
   the feminine line.

Answers

SMS, textos : dites « Je t'M » avec le pouce !

1 More than 92% of people in France own a mobile phone/In England more than a billion texts are sent each month/35 million greetings were texted on 1 January 2013 **3**

2 a) The young **1**
 b) Women use texts a bit more than men **1**
 c) Messages of love, friendship/and other functions to do with social relationships **2**

3 a) A circle of friends **1**
 b) A family member **1**
 c) New functions, such as access to the internet **1**

4 a) Shy people (people who are social phobics) **1**
 b) They have trouble communicating face to face/They avoid phone conversations and prefer texts/They like to have time to think about their answers (Any two) **2**

5 a) Older people or purists **1**
 b) Advantages: spelling as it sounds and letters to replace syllables **or** it increases the feeling of belonging to a group

Disadvantages: it limits the richness of discussion (language) **2**
 c) Don't forget to meet your friends for real and switch off your phone **2**

6 The author gives the impression of being in favour of texting: he talks about how popular and widespread it is/He talks about the positive things it is used for/He does mention the idea of addiction to texts, but then moves on/He talks about how use will continue to grow, without any negative comment/He discusses how texting can be of great value to shy people/He discusses how it simplifies communication/While he says some people see it as limiting, he then goes on to counter that with new developments **2**

Total **20**

7 In a few years, text messages or sms have conquered all mobile phone users!/To such an extent that the thumb has become/an organ of communication all by itself./Who would still send a love letter by post on Valentine's Day?/A text message is enough!

Dialogue 1
Society, problems

🔊 *Francine talks about young people and their attitude to drinking alcohol in France.*

Questions ❓

1 Does she think young French people drink like young Scottish and English people? **1**

....

2 How have things changed in French families at mealtimes? **2**

....

....

3 When do young French people drink now? **2**

....

....

4 What has changed for young French people? Give details. **2**

....

....

5 Why do young people not always go to cafés to meet their friends? **1**

....

6 Is the situation the same for boys and girls? Explain your answer. **2**

....

....

7 What horrifies her about drinking habits in Britain? **2**

....

....

Francine a parlé des jeunes en France et en Écosse.

Et toi, as-tu assez de liberté?

Que fais-tu le soir et le weekend?

Est-ce que la consommation de l'alcool est un problème pour les jeunes où tu habites?

Écris 120–150 mots en français pour exprimer tes idées.

Monologue 2
Society, family structures

🔊 *You hear this report about changes to family structures in France including 'PACS', civil partnerships.*

Questions ?

1 What has changed about the number of marriages over the last 100 years? **1**

....

2 What does the report define 'PACS' as? **1**

....

3 Why is 'PACS' considered revolutionary? **1**

....

4 How many marriages in France end in separation and divorce? **1**

....

5 What other fact does the report state about the rise in divorce? **1**

....

6 The speaker gives several pieces of information about single-parent families. State any **two**.

....

....

7 Overall, which statement best describes the speaker's opinion about the problem?
Tick (✓) the correct statement. **1**

She would like the number of divorces to come down.	
She thinks divorce harms children.	
She is giving a straightforward report of the facts.	

Dialogue 2
Society, family structures

🔊 *Sylvain talks about how he gets on with the other members of his family.*

Questions ❓

1 What does Sylvain tell you about his family? State any two things. **2**

....

....

2 Why does his father not live with him? **2**

....

....

3 How does he feel about it? **1**

....

4 When does he see his father? Give details. **2**

....

....

5 Why are things arranged the way they are? **2**

....

....

6 When does he see the grandparents who live further away? **1**

....

7 What does he tell you about his sister? State any two things. **2**

....

....

Sylvain parle de sa famille.

Et toi, tu t'entends bien avec ta famille?

Est-ce que ta famille est importante pour toi?

Préfères-tu sortir et parler avec tes copains?

Écris 120–150 mots en français pour exprimer tes idées.

Monologue 3
Learning, language learning

🔊 *You hear this report about the teaching of languages in French schools.*

Questions ❓

1 Who has launched a new plan? **1**

....

2 How many foreign languages should French pupils learn now? **1**

....

3 Where is the emphasis in primary and early secondary education? **1**

....

4 What should pupils be able to do by the end of primary school? **2**

....

....

5 What kind of situation should pupils at the end of lower secondary be able to get by in? **1**

....

6 What should a pupil at the end of their time at lycée be able to understand? **1**

....

7 Overall, which statement best describes the speaker's opinion about the situation?
Tick (✓) the correct statement. **1**

He is worried that French pupils are not good enough at languages.	
He is giving a straightforward report of the situation in French schools.	
He thinks there has been a huge improvement in French children's ability in languages.	

Dialogue 3
Learning, language learning

🔊 *Marie-Claire talks about learning languages at school.*

Questions ❓

1 What does Marie-Claire say when asked if she liked school? State two things. **2**

....

....

2 What was good about her first school? State any two things. **2**

....

....

3 How were her German and English teachers? Give details. **2**

....

....

4 What was her problem with her second school? State any two things. **2**

....

....

5 What else did she not like? State one thing. **1**

....

6 What was good about her second school? State two things. **2**

....

....

7 What was the best thing for her about the second school? **1**

....

Marie-Claire parle de ses écoles.

Et toi, est-ce que tu as aimé l'école?

Qu'est-ce que tu aimerais changer dans ton école?

Comment est ton voyage à l'école?

Écris 120–150 mots en français pour exprimer tes idées.

Monologue 4
Employability, careers

🔊 *You listen to a radio programme, where a girl who is training as a food technician has asked about how to start work.*

Questions ❓

1 What two things does the speaker say the girl might not have? **2**

....

....

2 What does she think the girl should consider doing? **1**

....

3 Why would this be important for her? **1**

....

4 What would be the ideal thing for the girl? **1**

....

5 What other possibilities are there for her? State two possibilities. **2**

....

....

6 Overall, which statement best describes the speaker's opinion about the girl's situation?
Tick (✓) the correct statement. **1**

She thinks the girl has to think very carefully about choosing the correct work.	
She thinks the girl will find it easy to get work once she has finished her training.	
She thinks having a part-time job will help her financially.	

Dialogue 4
Employability, careers

🔊 *Yvonne is being interviewed about her plans for the future.*

Questions ?

1 Where does Yvonne work part-time? Why does she work there? **2**

....

....

2 Give details about where she comes from. **2**

....

....

3 What does she tell you about her future plans? **2**

....

....

4 She discusses problems she has with her pupils in Scotland. State one of them. **1**

....

5 Why might she stay on in Scotland? **1**

....

6 Why does she think it would be possible for her to settle in Scotland? State two things. **2**

....

....

7 What do both of her parents think of this possibility? **2**

....

....

Yvonne parle de ses plans pour l'avenir.

Et toi, quels sont tes plans?

Aimerais-tu aller à l'université?

Veux-tu habiter et travailler à l'étranger?

Écris 120–150 mots en français pour exprimer tes idées.

Monologue 5
Employability, working

🔊 *You hear a radio programme giving advice to students on holiday jobs.*

Questions ❓

1   What two times are suitable for students to find jobs? **2**

    ....

    ....

2   What might the work help the students do? State one thing. **1**

    ....

3   Why might a student have to work? **1**

    ....

4   Where do employers look for holiday cover? **1**

    ....

5   What kind of employment is possible in certain regions? **1**

    ....

6   Where else might you look for a temporary job? **1**

    ....

7   Overall, which statement best describes the speaker's opinion about the employment
    situation? Tick (✔) the correct statement. **1**

Students should think hard about balancing work and study.	
It is often very difficult to find a temporary job.	
There is always work available if you want it.	

Monologue 2
Society, family structures

Answers

1 Dropped from 600,000 a year to 200,000 **1**
2 Civil union or contract between two people (to organise their life) **1**
3 It allows gay partnerships **1**
4 One in three **1**
5 People are divorcing earlier/sooner/**or** marriages are not lasting as long **1**
6 One person is in charge of the children/It is usually the mother/25% of families in France are single-parent families/Many children only see their father once a fortnight. One in four never see their father (Any two) **1**

7 **1**

She would like the number of divorces to come down.	
She thinks divorce harms children.	
She is giving a straightforward report of the facts.	✓

Dialogue 2
Society, family structures

Answers

1 Lives with his mum and sister/Grandparents live next door/Uncle, aunt and cousins live 30 metres away/Dad in the next village (Any two) **2**
2 It was not working/Parents were always fighting/Nobody was happy **2**
3 Would prefer if his dad was with them but accepts it **1**
4 After school (to do his homework)/The weekend to do things **2**
5 His dad is a teacher and can help with homework/His mum works late **2**
6 Summer holidays and Christmas **1**
7 She is young (eleven)/She is very funny/They don't argue/She often goes to their cousins' (Any two) **2**

Monologue 3
Learning, language learning

Answers

1 Education ministry **1**
2 Two **1**
3 Oral work **1**
4 Communicate simply (if their partner speaks slowly and clearly)/Exchange (simple) information **2**
5 Where they meet problems when travelling **1**
6 Essential information in a complex text **1**

7 **1**

He is worried that French pupils are not good enough at languages.	
He is giving a straightforward report of the situation in French schools.	✓
He thinks there has been a huge improvement in French children's ability in languages.	

Dialogue 3
Learning, language learning

1 Liked her first school/Thought her second school was awful **2**
2 Near her house/could have lunch at home/ Knew everyone in her class (Any two) **2**
3 Her German teacher was very sarcastic (looking for mistakes when they spoke)/ English teacher encouraged them to always speak English in class **2**
4 She had to take the train there/It was 20 kilometres away/She left home at 6.30 a.m. and got home at 7 p.m. (Any two) **2**

5 Her friends had gone to other schools/She felt isolated (lonely)/She didn't meet her classmates after school (Any one) **1**
6 She was in a European (bilingual) class/She did some subjects (history) in English)/She found it important to speak English well (Any two) **2**
7 She got good results **1**

Monologue 4
Employability, careers

1 Professional experience/Not yet got her qualification (diploma) **2**
2 Get a part-time job **1**
3 Without experience it will be hard to get a job when she is finished **1**
4 Finding a company that would employ her at the end, if they liked her **1**
5 Working in a market/Job in a supermarket/ a fast food place **2**

6

She thinks the girl has to think very carefully about choosing the correct work.	✓	**1**
She thinks the girl will find it easy to get work once she has finished her training.		
She thinks having a part-time job will help her financially.		

Dialogue 4

Employability, careers

Answers

1 She works in a bar/To get to know people **2**
2 A village in the north of France/Half an hour (30 km) from Lille **2**
3 She will go home to finish her studies/Then come back to Scotland to become a teacher **2**
4 Some of them refuse to speak in class/Others ask why they have to learn French (Either one) **1**

5 Her boyfriend is here **1**
6 Glasgow is not unlike Lille/Flights home are not expensive **2**
7 Her mother would prefer her to stay in France/Her father is happy (because he loves golf and can play whenever he comes) **2**

Monologue 5

Employability, working

Answers

1 Winter holidays/Summer holidays **2**
2 Spend money in the sales/Pay towards their studying (Either one) **1**
3 Not all parents can afford to support them **1**
4 Job agencies **1**
5 Agricultural (picking fruit and vegetables) **1**
6 Café or restaurant **1**

7

		1
Students should think hard about balancing work and study.		
It is often very difficult to find a temporary job.	✓	
There is always work available if you want it.		

Dialogue 5

Employability, working

Answers

1 She works in a bar/Thursdays from 8 till 12/8 hours on Saturdays (Any two) **2**
2 She is an assistant in a school/and her flat is expensive **2**
3 It is well paid/She gets to meet people **2**
4 On Fridays/She is tired when she has to go to school **2**

5 She stayed at home/didn't have to pay for rent and food (Either one) **1**
6 In the summer holidays/(An assistant) in a holiday camp **2**
7 Seeing the children enjoy themselves **1**

Monologue 6
Culture, working abroad

Answers

1 Nearly 600,000 **1**
2 Fed up of unemployment/Looking for more interesting careers **2**
3 Things being better (the best) **1**
4 A spirit of adventure **1**
5 He thought he was being exploited in his job at the time/**or** He dreamt of leaving **1**
6 He couldn't find any interesting work/ He was not prepared enough (Either one) **1**

7

		1
She thinks it is a great chance for people to expand their horizons.		
She thinks it is much easier to find work abroad than in France.		
She thinks you have to weigh up very carefully the pros and cons of going abroad to work.	✓	

Dialogue 6
Culture, working abroad

Answers

1 The weather/It is colder and rains more (Either one) **1**
2 France: coffee or hot chocolate with bread (and cereal)/Scotland: hamburger or sausages, eggs and ham (bacon) **2**
3 Couldn't eat it/he would hate it **1**
4 Most people keep working and have a drink and a sandwich/Others go jogging and eat something quickly **2**
5 They eat sandwiches or chips in the street/They don't sit down **2**
6 He went home for a meal made by his mother **1**
7 He takes an hour/eats a main course and pudding **1**
8 Most French restaurants offer French food/Hardly any restaurants in Scotland have Scottish food **or** Curry seems to be the main Scottish dish **2**

Dialogue 1
Society, problems

Francine talks about young people and their attitude to drinking alcohol in France.

Question : Francine, j'ai entendu que les jeunes en France ont commencé à boire l'alcool comme les britanniques : est-ce que vous avez remarqué cela vous-même ?

Francine : Il ne faut pas exagérer ! Rien en France ressemble aux rues d'une grande ville en Angleterre ou l'Écosse le samedi soir. Mais bien sûr, les jeunes ont tendance à boire entre eux maintenant plus qu'avant.

Question : Est-ce qu'on a encore l'habitude comme dans les autres générations d'apprendre à boire en famille ?

Francine : Je crois moins : autrefois les petits enfants prenaient un verre de vin mixé avec de l'eau à table le soir, mais maintenant on est plus conscient de la santé des enfants, et on leur offre du jus de fruit ou de l'eau à table.

Question : Alors les jeunes Français ne boivent plus du vin à table ?

Francine : Mais si, mais surtout à des fêtes de famille, ou pour les occasions exceptionnelles, comme les anniversaires, les mariages, des choses comme ça. Et même là, on commence plus tard, les enfants sont plus âgés, ils ont au moins douze/treize ans maintenant.

Question : Vous avez dit que les jeunes boivent entre eux : qu'est-ce que ça veut dire ?

Francine : Autrefois les jeunes avaient moins de liberté, ils devaient rester à la maison le soir après six heures, six heures et demie du soir. Maintenant ils peuvent sortir le soir : c'est là qu'ils s'achètent des bières pour boire ensemble.

Question : Ils ne vont pas au café ?

Francine : Pas forcément : les cafés, ça coûte assez cher et puis ce n'est pas très privé, les jeunes ne peuvent pas être entre eux. Donc on va au supermarché, on achète quelques cannettes de bière, et on va au parc.

Question : C'est vrai pour les filles comme pour les garçons ?

Francine : Dans une certaine mesure : les filles n'ont pas encore autant de liberté que les garçons, elles doivent rentrer plus tôt, puis elles font mieux leurs devoirs que les garçons, mais si, on voit aussi des fois des filles dans les parcs !

⇨

→

Question : Mais ce n'est pas comme ici en Grande Bretagne ?

Francine : Ah non, ici on voit les jeunes totalement ivres, beaucoup plus jeunes qu'en France, les jeunes quelquefois de douze/treize ans, et en plus ils ne boivent pas de la bière, ils boivent de la vodka, des boissons fortement alcoolisées. On les trouve inconscients dans les rues, quelquefois.

Monologue 2
Society, family structures
You hear this report about changes to family structures in France over the last hundred years.

Depuis les années 20, le nombre de mariages est passé d'environ 600 milles mariages par an à 200 milles. L'âge du premier mariage aussi a augmenté. Elle est passée d'environ 24 ans à 28 ans. Une alternative ? Il existe aussi une alternative, le PACS (Pacte Civil de Solidarité), une sorte d'union civile. C'est un contrat entre deux personnes (les partenaires), qui leur permet d'organiser leur vie commune. Cette alternative au mariage est en quelque sorte « révolutionnaire », car elle autorise l'union de personnes homosexuelles.

Le taux de divorce augmente chaque année et les chiffres sont là pour le prouver : en France, un mariage sur trois se termine par une séparation. En plus ces divorces interviennent de plus en plus tôt, parce que les mariages durent de moins en moins longtemps.

Une famille monoparentale est une famille constituée d'un seul adulte et d'au moins un enfant, alors des familles où un seul parent a la charge des enfants. Le plus souvent c'est la mère (après un divorce ou une séparation). Le gouvernement a estimé que 25 % des familles sont monoparentales, et, que beaucoup des enfants séparés voient leur père tous les 15 jours, un enfant sur quatre pas du tout.

Dialogue 2
Society, family structures

Sylvain talks about how he gets on with the other members of his family.

Question : Sylvain, vous avez une grande famille ?

Sylvain : Alors, oui et non. J'habite chez ma mère et ma sœur dans un petit village, mais mes grands-parents habitent à côté, mon oncle, ma tante et mes cousines à trente mètres, et mon père dans le prochain village.

Question : Vous l'aimez comme ça ?

Sylvain : Eh bien, je l'aurais préféré que mon père habite encore chez nous, mais ça ne marchait plus, mes parents bagarraient tout le temps, et personne n'était heureu. Donc il y a quatre ans il a trouvé une nouvelle maison et voilà. Je l'accepte.

Question : Vous le voyez souvent ?

Sylvain : Ah oui, normalement j'y vais après l'école et je fais mes devoirs là. Je rentre pour dîner. Le weekend on sort souvent ensemble : ou on fait du bowling, ou on va au cinéma le soir.

Question : Vous seulement ?

Sylvain : Ah non, ma sœur Marie vient aussi : mon père est professeur, donc il peut aider avec les devoirs, et ma mère doit travailler plus tard, donc c'est très convenable pour tout le monde.

Question : Et comment vous vous entendez avec vos grands-parents ?

Sylvain : Les grands-parents qui habitent à côté de nous, ce sont les parents de ma mère, et on se voit beaucoup. Je les aime bien, mais ils sont assez sévères, donc je préfère aller chez mon père. Mes autres grands-parents je vois rarement, car ils habitent loin de chez nous, mais on leur rend visite à Noël et pendant les grandes vacances. C'est super chez eux, et ils ne sont pas du tout sévères, on s'amuse très bien là.

Question : Vous vous entendez, vous et votre sœur ?

Sylvain : Ah oui : elle est assez jeune, elle a onze ans, mais elle est très rigolo, et on ne se dispute jamais. Elle est aussi souvent chez nos cousins.

Monologue 3
Learning, language learning

You hear this report about the teaching of languages in French schools.

Le ministère de l'Éducation nationale a lancé un plan de rénovation de l'enseignement des langues vivantes étrangères qui concerne tous les élèves de l'école élémentaire au lycée. L'objectif de ce plan est d'améliorer le niveau des élèves dans deux langues étrangères.

Les nouveaux programmes de langues vivantes étrangères à l'école primaire et au collège trouvent l'oral plus important au cours de leur éducation. De nombreuses initiatives ont été lancées pour renforcer l'exposition des élèves à la langue.

À la fin de l'enseignement primaire les élèves doivent communiquer de façon simple si l'interlocuteur parle lentement et distinctement. Ils peuvent aussi échanger des informations simples sur des sujets familiers et habituels.

À la fin du collège les élèves doivent se débrouiller dans la plupart des situations rencontrées en voyage, raconter un événement, une expérience, et défendre une idée.

À la fin du lycée un élève doit comprendre l'essentiel d'un sujet concret ou abstrait dans un texte complexe, et participer dans une discussion technique dans sa spécialité avec un degré de spontanéité et d'aisance. Il peut donner un avis sur un sujet d'actualité et en débattre.

Dialogue 3
Learning, language learning
Marie-Claire talks about learning languages at school.

Question : Marie-Claire, est-ce que vous aimiez vos jours aller à l'école ?

Marie-Claire : Alors là, j'ai deux réponses : mon collège, je l'aimais bien, mais lorsque je suis allée au lycée à l'âge de quinze ans, j'ai trouvé ça affreux, et je n'étais pas du tout contente de devoir y aller.

Question : Pourquoi aimiez-vous votre collège ?

Marie-Claire : Eh bien, c'était tout près de la maison : nous habitions à cinq cent mètres du collège, donc je pouvais rentrer à midi pour déjeuner chez moi, et je connaissais très bien tout le monde dans ma classe.

Question : Vous aimiez aussi les professeurs ?

Marie-Claire : Oui, ils étaient presque tous gentils, à part ma prof d'allemand : elle était très sarcastique, et aimait trouver les fautes quand on parlait en classe. Mais mon prof d'anglais était complètement différent : il nous encourageait tous à parler en anglais tout le temps en classe.

Question : Et pourquoi le lycée était-il une expérience moins positive ?

Marie-Claire : Ben, d'abord je devais prendre le train pour y aller, car c'était à vingt kilomètres de chez moi, ce qui voulait dire que je devais quitter la maison à six heures et demie, manger à la cantine, puis je ne rentrais le soir qu'à dix-neuf heures, et il me restait des devoirs à faire.

Question : Mais à part ça ?

Marie-Claire : Presque tous mes copains sont allés dans un autre lycée, donc je me sentais assez isolée, car je voyageais seule le matin, et je ne rencontrais pas les autres lycéens après les cours.

Question : Mais vous êtes quand même restée là-bas ?

Marie-Claire : Eh bien je voulais le faire, parce que j'étais dans une classe Européene ou bilingue, on faisait quelques matières en anglais comme par exemple l'histoire, et puis ça j'appréciais beaucoup, parce que je trouvais ça important de bien parler anglais. ⇨

Question : C'était un bon lycée ?

Marie-Claire : Ah oui, bien sûr, et les profs étaient intéressants, et puis j'ai beaucoup appris, et le plus important c'est que j'ai obtenu un bon bac, j'avais de bonnes notes : le problème était plutôt la distance et tout ce que cela voulait dire pour moi.

Monologue 4
Employability, careers

You listen to a radio programme, where a girl who is training as a food technician has asked about how to start work.

Comment commencer dans le monde du travail?

Si vous avez une formation en technicien de contrôle de qualité alimentaire, mais n'avez aucune autre expérience professionnelle et n'avez pas encore reçu votre diplôme, vous pourriez penser à faire un boulot à temps partiel. Quel type de boulot pouvez-vous faire?

Pour vous lancer dans le domaine, on vous conseille de chercher soit un contrat à temps partiel, soit un stage, dans une société liée au contrôle qualité alimentaire. C'est important car une expérience vous sera nécessaire à la fin de votre formation pour obtenir une poste permanente, c'est-à-dire un contrat de travail, parce que les entreprises n'embauchent pas les personnes sans expérience maintenant.

Idéalement vous pouvez trouver du travail chez une société qui te promet un contrat à la fin, s'ils sont contents de vous.

Vous pouvez aussi travailler sur un marché. Là, on recrute en permanence et vous restez comme ça dans l'alimentaire. Bien sûr il y a aussi les petits boulots en hypermarchés, McDonald et compagnie, mais essayez de trouver quelque chose, car sinon, à la fin de vos études vous allez vous retrouver dans une situation difficile et risquez de ne pas trouver de boulot dans votre domaine sans avoir d'expérience.

Dialogue 4
Employability, careers
Yvonne is being interviewed about her plans for the future.

Question : Yvonne, vous travaillez à présent à Glasgow : qu'est-ce que vous faites exactement ?

Yvonne : D'abord, je suis venue ici pour un an comme assistante dans une école à Glasgow, et ensuite j'ai pris un poste comme serveuse dans un bar, afin de pouvoir rencontrer d'autres jeunes gens.

Question : Vous êtes d'où en France ?

Yvonne : Je suis étudiante en fac à Lille, mais je suis originaire d'un petit village dans le Nord, Marchiennes, tout près de Lille, pour préciser à trente kilomètres, ou une demi-heure dans le train.

Question : Vous comptez retourner en France bientôt ?

Yvonne : Oui, bien sûr : je veux reprendre mes études en septembre, et ensuite je resterai encore deux ans pour en finir, mais après j'ai l'intention de revenir en Écosse avec l'intention de devenir professeur.

Question : Alors vous aimez les enfants en Écosse, évidemment ceux dans votre école ?

Yvonne : Ah oui, la plupart oui : il y en a qui m'offrent des problèmes de temps en temps, alors ils refusent de parler dans la classe et bien sûr il y a ceux qui me demandent tout le temps « Pourquoi est-ce que je dois apprendre le français ? », mais j'ai beaucoup d'élèves qui s'intéressent pour la France, et voudraient y aller.

Question : Est-ce que vous comptez rester longtemps en Écosse, dès votre retour ici ?

Yvonne : Là, je ne sais pas : ça dépend de comment ça se déroule avec mon petit ami. J'ai rencontré quelqu'un ici, et si ça continue, donc je veux bien rester longtemps.

Question : Vous pourriez imaginer de créer une famille ici ?

Yvonne : Oui, bien sûr. Vous savez, Glasgow n'est pas tellement différente de Lille, et puis il y a des vols de l'Écosse à Lille ou en Belgique qui ne sont pas du tout chers, donc comme ça je pourrai rester en contact avec ma famille.

Question : Qu'est-ce qu'en pensent vos parents ?

⇨

Yvonne : Alors, pour ma mère, naturellement elle préférerait
que je resterais en France, plus proche d'elle, mais elle
accepte mes désirs, et mon père est fanatiqe de golf,
donc pour lui, il est content, car comme ça il peut venir
n'importe quand faire un petit tour de golf !

Monologue 5
Employability, working
You hear a radio programme giving advice to students on holiday jobs.

Pour les étudiants, les vacances sont souvent l'occasion de petits
boulots pour gagner un peu d'argent. Grandes vacances, vacances
d'hiver, c'est le moment pour les jeunes de trouver un boulot de
quelques semaines ou quelques jours pour pouvoir ensuite dépenser
de l'argent aux soldes, ou tout simplement payer les études. Mais les
boulots d'étudiants ne sont pas si faciles à trouver.

La vie d'étudiant n'est pas toujours facile, elle a un coût que
malheureusement tous les parents ne peuvent pas supporter, alors
l'étudiant doit gagner lui aussi de l'argent. Pour les grandes vacances,
les entreprises recherchent parfois des remplaçants pour les
vacances, et passent souvent par les sociétés de travail temporaire ;
pensez à vous inscrire chez ces agences, pour trouver plus facilement
du travail.

Pour les régions productrices de fruits et légumes, il est aussi
possible d'aller auprès des agriculteurs pour du travail physique
de ramassage ou d'emballage. Les restaurants ou cafés recrutent
parfois aussi durant l'été, des périodes où leur activité explose, donc
il existe l'occasion de trouver un contrat de travail durant les grandes
vacances. Les étudiants qui désirent travailler peuvent également
trouver plusieurs ressources intéressantes sur le net. Les boulots
d'étudiants sont très recherchés, pour participer aux frais d'études,
se payer le permis de conduire, une voiture, ou s'offrir quelques

vacances. Les offres d'emploi pourtant sont limitées, et le travail proposé est parfois difficile et souvent pas bien payé. Les étudiants doivent donc être très motivés, et chercher leur emploi avec conviction pour être choisis parmi le grand nombre de candidats qui souhaitent également gagner de l'argent durant les vacances.

Dialogue 5
Employability, working
Yvonne talks about her part-time job.

Question : Yvonne, vous travaillez le soir ou le weekend ?

Yvonne : Oui, les deux. Je travaille dans un bar les jeudis de 8h jusqu'à minuit, puis aussi les samedis pour huit heures en totale.

Question : Pourquoi est-ce que vous faîtes ce travail ?

Yvonne : Alors, il y a deux raisons : premièrement, je suis assistante dans une école à Glasgow, et mon appartement est très cher, donc je trouve que j'ai besoin de gagner un peu d'argent en plus. Et puis, ce qui est plus important, je peux sortir et rencontrer d'autres gens dans une bonne ambiance.

Question : Vous aimez votre petit boulot ?

Yvonne : Bien sûr : c'est bien payé. En plus je rencontre beaucoup de monde lorsque je suis dans le bar, et après le travail on sort pour aller à un club ensemble.

Question : Il n'y a pas de problèmes avec le travail ?

Yvonne : Eh oui, je dois admettre que le vendredi, quand je dois me lever tôt pour aller à l'école, je suis très fatiguée et il me faut beaucoup d'énergie avec mes classes. Et quelquefois il y a des gens qui ont trop bu dans le bar, et ça peut être gênant, mais c'est assez rare, quand même.

Question : Est-ce que vous avez travaillé chez vous en France, pendant que vous étiez en fac ?

Yvonne : Non, pas vraiment. J'habite encore chez mes parents, et pour cette raison je n'ai pas de loyer à payer, non plus pour manger. L'université est à deux kilomètres, donc le transport ne coûte pas cher.

Question : Alors vous vivez de votre argent de poche ?

Yvonne : Ah non, je travaille toujours pendant les grandes vacances, et je garde l'argent que je gagne : ça me donne normalement tout l'argent qu'il me faut pour l'année universitaire.

Question : Qu'est-ce que vous faîtes comme travail ?

Yvonne : Je suis monitrice dans une colonie de vacances. Je fais celà pendant les mois de juillet et d'août. C'est génial, parce que tout est payé, ma chambre, les repas, et je ne dépense rien, seulement mon phone portable.

Question : Qu'est-ce que vous devez faire dans le travail ?

Yvonne : Alors, on travaille avec les enfants qui sont là pendant quatre semaines. Les enfants avec lesquels je travaille ont entre six et douze ans. On leur offre des activités sportives et culturelles, on reste avec eux quand ils mangent, on écoute leurs problèmes entre beaucoup d'autres devoirs : c'est fatigant, mais il en vaut la peine, quand on voit les petits s'amuser tellement.

Monologue 6
Culture, working abroad
You hear a podcast about French people who choose to live and work abroad.

D'après les chiffres annoncés récemment, en dix ans, près de 600 milles Français sont partis à la recherche d'un emploi à l'étranger. Et encore ! L'ambassade de France en Chine annonçait récemment une hausse du pourcentage des jeunes expatriés (près de 100 chaque mois) venus s'installer définitivement, soit à la recherche d'un job d'été, d'un stage, ou d'un emploi. Travailler à l'étranger attire donc de plus en plus de jeunes diplomés affligés par le chômage en France ou attirés par des perspectives de carrières plus intéressantes que dans leur pays. ⇒

D'un autre côté aussi, il y a les personnes professionnelles qui espèrent le meilleur à l'étranger. Et bien évidemment, il y a des travailleurs, qui de plus en plus, trouvent intéressant l'idée d'aller voir plus loin, dans un nouvel environnement pour redynamiser leur carrière. Bien sûr, travailler à l'étranger est une décision qui mérite d'être prise avec beaucoup de soin. Seul le goût de l'aventure ne suffit plus.

Un travailleur qui regrette sa décision explique : « J'avais l'impression d'être exploité dans mon travail ici. En plus, je rêvais de partir à l'étranger. Je me disais qu'ailleurs, surtout dans un pays exotique, j'aurai plus de chances de me faire remarquer. J'ai donc réuni mes économies et j'ai fait le grand saut. Malheureusement, je n'ai rien trouvé d'intéressant. J'avais une période difficile qui finalement m'a fait admettre que je n'avais pas été assez préparé. Je suis revenu au pays déçu. ».

Dialogue 6
Culture, working abroad
Vincent talks about the differences between eating in France and in Scotland.

Question : Vincent, vous êtes depuis un an ici en Écosse. Quelles sont pour vous les différences les plus marquantes entre la vie ici et la vie chez vous ?

Vincent : Je viens d'une ville dans le Midi, donc évidemment la différence la plus importante est le temps. Ici il pleut souvent, et il fait beaucoup plus froid, même en été. Mais à part celà, je dirais que la plus grande différence est la façon de se nourrir.

Question : Vous pouvez expliquer un peu ?

Vincent : Ça commence avec le petit déjeuner. Chez nous, on prend un café ou un bol de chocolat avec du pain. On peut aussi trouver des céréales. Mais ici j'ai vu des gens commencer la journée avec un hamburger, ou un grand plat plein de saucissons, d'œufs au jambon. Puis je vois d'autres qui ne prennent rien sauf un coca.

Question : Vous l'avez essayé vous-même, le petit déjeuner anglais ?

Vincent : Ah non, je ne le pourrais pas faire. J'ai déjà horreur des aliments trop gras, et le matin ça serait pire.

Question : Il y a d'autres différences ?

Vincent : Je dirais qu'il n'y a que des différences : à midi, pour déjeuner ici, la plupart de ceux que je rencontre ne s'arrêtent pas de travailler. Ils restent au bureau

64

avec un sandwich et un boisson, peut-être ils regardent un peu sur l'internet, mais c'est tout. Il y a d'autres qui sortent pour faire du jogging, et après ils mangent vite quelque chose pendant deux/trois minutes. Même les élèves des écoles dans les alentours, je les vois dans la rue à midi avec un sandwich ou des frites à la main, ils ne s'asseyent même.

Question : Et ce n'est pas votre habitude ?

Vincent : Bien sûr que non ! Quand j'étais au lycée, on avait une heure et demie pour déjeuner, et j'en profitais pour rentrer chez moi et manger dans tout confort quelque chose qu'avait préparée ma mère.

Question : Et qu'est-ce que vous faîtes ici en Écosse ?

Vincent : Alors, on a une heure pour le déjeuner et je prends cette heure, je n'en sacrificie rien au travail, je me relâche. Je mange un plat cuisiné et un dessert, et après je prends un café. Je reste Français !

Question : Comment trouvez-vous les restaurants ici ?

Vincent : Là aussi je vois beaucoup de différences. Chez nous, la plupart des restaurants offrent un repas français, quoi. Il y a bien sûr des restaurants italiens et vietnamiens ou chinois, mais c'est à peu près tout. Ici, on a des difficultés à trouver un restaurant qui offre des plats écossais. Le plat principal écossais me semble être un curry.

Question : Qu'est-ce que vous en pensez ?

Vincent : Pour moi, je suis content : je peux expérimenter avec un tas de cuisines différentes : ici j'ai mangé pour la première fois dans un restaurant méxicain, et je mange regulièrement dans un restaurant végétarien, chose que je ne ferais jamais chez nous, même si ça existait.

Monologue 7
Culture, travel

You hear this report about holiday planning.

Partir en vacances est toujours enthousiasmant. Partir à l'étranger peut être source d'une légère anxiété. Préparer, prévoir et organiser son voyage évitera le stress de dernière minute et vous épargnera des soucis pendant cette belle période que sont les vacances. Quelques séances de natation, un peu de vélo, de marche à pieds, tout sera bon pour habituer vos muscles à l'exercice physique que vous pratiquerez pendant vos vacances, car si vous vous lancez sans entraînement, vous risquez votre santé.

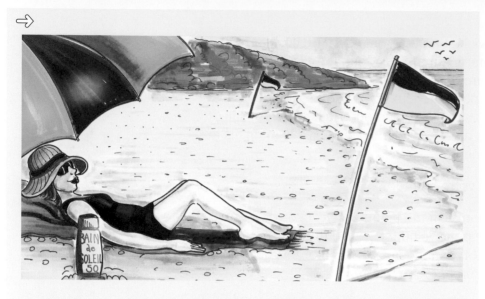

Attention ! Les méfaits du soleil ne se limitent pas aux coups de soleil. Il accentue les rides, il favorise le vieillissement du peau et pire, il peut être à l'origine de cancers de la peau. Protégez votre corps d'un T-shirt léger, d'un chapeau, vos yeux de lunettes de soleil de qualité. Ne faites pas trop confiance aux crèmes solaires. Certaines d'entre elles sont plus dangereuses que le soleil lui-même, à cause des produits cancérigènes qui les composent. D'autre part, elles vous donnent l'illusion que vous êtes bien protégé et vous poussent à passer trop de temps sous le soleil. Il est aussi important d'éviter les heures chaudes du milieu de journée.

Chaque année, des noyades transforment les vacances en tragédies. Il faut rester prudent, obéir aux consignes de sécurité sur les plages, respecter les couleurs des drapeaux rouges et verts sur la plage. Que ce soit à la mer ou en eau douce, entrez toujours progressivement dans l'eau. Mouillez-vous les bras, et si elle vous semble trop froide, sortez de l'eau. Evitez de nager seul.

Dialogue 7
Culture, travel

Jacques talks about his experiences of holidays with his family and his friends.

Question : Jacques, quand êtes-vous parti en vacances sans les parents pour la première fois ?

Jacques : Alors, ça dépend : je suis parti pratiquement chaque année dès l'âge de treize ans en colonie de vacances avec mes copains, normalement dans le midi. Là, c'était une visite organisée, il y avait des moniteurs, ce n'était pas vraiment indépendant. La première fois je suis parti avec mes copains indépendamment, j'avais dix-sept ans.

Question : Où êtes-vous allés ?

⇒

Jacques : On est allés en Bretagne à vélo pour faire du camping, et on a passé une semaine près de Saint Malo. Nous étions quatre, tous en première au lycée. On a fait cinquante kilomètres par jour, mais nous restions toujours près de la mer, pour pouvoir nager chaque matin.

Question : Comment est-ce que ça vous a plu ?

Jacques : C'était super : on s'est levé tard le matin, il n'y avait pas de pression pour visiter les monuments, et nous avons mangé quand et comment nous voulions.

Question : Vous aimiez aller en vacances avec vos parents ?

Jacques : Ah oui, je m'entends bien avec ma famille, et on allait toujours à une petite maison dans le midi, au bord de la mer. J'avais beaucoup de liberté, parce qu'on connaissait tout le monde dans le village, et j'avais des amis là-bas.

Question : Il n'y avait jamais de problèmes ?

Jacques : Si, il y avait des règlements pour les repas : je devais me lever à huit heures pour le petit déjeuner, et je devais toujour rentrer à une heure pour déjeuner, même si je voulais rester à la plage avec mes copains.

Question : Comment sont vos vacances aujourd'hui ?

Jacques : C'est bien varié : quelquefois je pars en train avec mes parents une semaine à la même maison, dans le midi, mais je pars aussi avec ma petite amie un peu plus loin. On part en avion, pour aller en Grèce ou en Espagne.

Question : Êtes-vous actif en vacances ?

Jacques : Oui, bien que j'aime encore me lever tard. Mais je suis assez sportif, et j'aime pratiquer de nouveaux sports. L'année dernière j'ai appris la plongée sous-marine, et cette année je veux bien pratiquer de la planche à voile.

Introduction

Talking is worth **25 per cent** of your overall Higher result. You will have to carry out only one Talking assessment, possibly in the spring term. This assessment will consist of a presentation by you, with a follow-up discussion with your teacher on this and related topics. The topic for the presentation will be agreed by you and your teacher together, and the whole assessment will be marked by your teacher. It will be recorded, and may be sent off to SQA for assessment/moderation, or it may not. You will not know in advance whether it will be sent off, so just assume it will be. You will also be assessed in talking in the Using Language Unit. How you will be assessed for this will be decided by your school or teacher, as there is no set way for this to happen.

You and your teacher should discuss the topic area you want to use for your presentation. You should choose an area you are comfortable with, but one that allows you to display your knowledge of French, and gives some chance to put in some good vocabulary and structures. This presentation will be worth 10 marks, or 10 per cent of your final award. You will start off the discussion in this topic area, but will move on to one or more other topic areas you have covered during the Higher Course. The discussion will be worth 15 marks, or 15 per cent of your final award. There will be a further 5 marks for 'sustaining the conversation'.

The rules for the assessment are quite clear: there will be a presentation, lasting about two minutes, which gives you a chance to start off the assessment well and confidently. You will have to speak with a certain number of words (*five headings of up to eight words each*) allowed as notes to help you through. Your presentation will be graded according to the criteria shown in Appendix 3, and that will let you see what is expected of you at each of the possible marks.

The second part of the assessment will be a discussion, which will cover topic areas you have looked at over the course of your Higher French studies. The discussion will normally last up to six minutes. This discussion will be marked following the same criteria as the presentation, but there will also be an additional 5 possible marks for sustaining the conversation.

In this chapter we will look at the two types of task in detail, and give you advice and support on preparing for the kind of task you are facing.

The presentation

For this assessment, just as for the prepared talk at National 5, you will have to talk on a subject of your choice for up to two minutes. You can prepare this well in advance, and learn it so that you can be absolutely sure of what you have to do. You should also think carefully about your learning style, and whether a selection of words to use as notes to guide you through your presentation is the way to go, or just learning by heart. Some people find it useful to have five cue cards, each with a number of words to jog the memory. Others find that the first eight words of each section work best. It is important you find your own style.

You must be reasonably accurate in your use of French, and use tenses and a variety of structures well. You are expected to expand beyond the kind of vocabulary and ideas you used at National 5. The presentation should have a clear structure, with a beginning and an end. Your opinions are very important, and you should also include reasons for some of these opinions. You can see examples of this later on in this chapter.

Planning your talk

When you have a subject for your assessment, try to break it down into three to five sections, and prepare each one separately: this will make it easier to remember, as well as giving you structure. You are allowed five headings of eight words each as support, so these key words should help you into each section of your talk. This is handy as, if you get nervous and you get a bit mixed up in one part, you can recover in the next part with the help of your key words.

Once you've chosen your topic area, focus on the actual language you will use. Below you will find a few dos and don'ts.

Hints & tips ★

✓ **Do** look at the texts you have been working from for good ideas you can use. These texts will be at the level you should be working at.

✓ **Do** make sure you understand what you are saying, or it will be very difficult to remember it properly. Use complex language, yes, but only language you are comfortable with.

✓ **Do** think about your pronunciation: record yourself and listen to what you sound like. Could you sound more French?

✓ **Do** share your drafts with your teacher to get any suggestions or corrections made, and do this well in advance.

✓ **Do** use a variety of structures. Start collecting these in a notebook or in an area of your folder or computer.

✓ **Do** vary your tenses, and put in complex sentences, using a variety of different joining words or conjunctions like parce que, car or quand. If you can, use some of the conjunctions followed by the subjunctive (advice on this is in the structures and vocabulary chapter, Chapter 12).

⇨

⇨

✓ **Do** give your opinion at every opportunity, and work at having different ways of saying what you think. Look at the 'Giving opinions and reasons' section in the chapter on structures and vocabulary (Chapter 12, page 92).

✓ **Do** also use adjectives and adverbs, some of these attached to the nouns and verbs they are describing.

✓ **Don't** leave the preparation to the last minute. If you start your preparation early, you'll be able to ask your teacher for advice on any vocabulary or grammar you're unsure of. That means not just the week before, but a month before.

✓ **Don't** always stick to safe, simple language. It may be easier, but won't get the best grades. Try out some of the more impressive sentences you've come across. Note down useful vocabulary and phrases you've seen elsewhere under appropriate topic headings so you can reuse them in your talking tests.

✓ Just as at National 5, **don't** use lists of things, such as school subjects, places in town or favourite foods to try to make your talk longer: this will count against you.

Choosing a topic

The topic areas from which you will be working are the topic areas of the Higher Course, which are in Appendix 1. Although the presentation and initial part of the conversation will be on this area, you need to be able to deal with other areas, as the conversation should go into at least one other area, and you must be prepared. Discuss with your teacher how this will go, but remember you will not be expected to cover areas you have not yet dealt with in class as part of your Higher Course.

How should you choose a topic? There are several points you should think about:

Hints & tips

✓ Choose a topic area you are comfortable with, and know something about.

✓ Make sure your chosen area allows you to get in a variety of tenses and structures, and allows you to put in opinions and feelings and explain the reasons for these opinions.

✓ Make sure it is not too simple, and only allows you to use the kind of language that would be appropriate for National 5: this is a particular danger with topics like family and school. Your daily routine, or what you are studying at school, are not able to give you enough chance to express yourself.

✓ You might want to choose the topic area you have been dealing with most recently, as it will be fresh in your mind.

✓ You might want to base your presentation on a small area of a topic you have dealt with, allowing you to talk about this area in a wider context in the conversation. In health, for instance, you could talk about the fact that so many girls smoke, and what can be done about it. This means you can go on to talk about diet, problems with drinking and drugs.

Let us look at some possible presentations, one from each topic area. The next section will guide you through the process involved in preparing for and carrying out the assessment for three specific topics. You can follow the same pattern, for a presentation of your own choice. You should also look at the chapters on writing (Chapters 10 and 11) for further help on different specific areas and the transcripts in Chapter 8 for the kind of language to use.

Presentation topics
1 Le tabagisme et les jeunes

This topic comes from the Society context, and covers an aspect of young people's problems. Using this as a presentation will allow you to speak in both the first and the third person, give opinions and justify these and use good phrases from the texts you are working from. It should also allow you to give conflicting points of view.

Your first task should be a kind of brainstorming: look at your source texts and select a variety of really good phrases or ideas. Look at these in turn, and try to identify a pattern or storyline to follow and give your presentation some structure. Then, break your task into areas. You could start with a section in which you talk about the importance of health, then have a section in which you talk about the dangers that smoking poses (and include a reference to what you think yourself), move on to where there are problems with this and finish off with what people (and you) should be doing to improve things. If you have a textbook, you could use this for source material, or you could look on the internet for supporting material. You should also look at the chapter on personal response writing (Chapter 11) for further help on different specific areas.

The first section might sound something like this:

DÉFENSE DE FUMER

De nos jours, l'on parle beaucoup de l'importance de la santé pour les jeunes : on pense à la nourriture dans les cantines scolaires, on essaie d'interdire aux gens de fumer dans les lieux publics, il y a beaucoup de publicité à la télévision et au cinéma pour persuader aux gens d'arrêter de fumer.

This allows you to introduce the topic, and can also serve as the lead in to later questions in the conversation. It also is general, and so avoids using *je* for just now. The second section can then let you move from the general to the particular. Here is an example:

> Il est important de penser aux dangers pour les jeunes qui pensent à fumer, et une des choses les plus importantes est de leur persuader de ne pas commencer. Lorsqu'on commence, il est souvent difficile d'arreter. Après, ça coûte cher, car les cigarettes prennent tout son argent, et parce qu'on pue le vieux tabac, personne ne veut s'asseoir à côté de vous.

This has allowed you to give opinions, and justify them. You also have put in a sub-clause and some adjectives and adverbs.

The next section allows you to give some structure by moving to problems, to the other side of the discussion and also to personalise the discussion:

> Je le trouve quelquefois assez difficile d'éviter le tabac : souvent j'ai des amis qui veulent expérimenter, et je ne veux pas les perdre. Des fois quand je sors avec mes copains, il y en a un ou deux qui fument et boivent trop de bière, et je n'ai plus envie de sortir. Je préfère dans ce cas rester à la maison.

You have left in some hints for where the later discussion can go: drinking or peer pressure. It is important to add in the little words and phrases that make your French flow better; words like *quand même*, *quelquefois* and *assez*.

For the final section, you need to come to a conclusion, as well as giving an answer to the problems in the third paragraph. In this section it is the chance to show off all your ways of expressing opinions and making demands:

> Personnellement, je trouve qu'il vaut mieux montrer dans les classes les poumons des personnes qui fument, pour voir exactement les effets sur son corps. Je sais que beaucoup de jeunes y ferment les yeux, mais il faut tout de même persister, car la santé est tellement importante pour notre avenir : il serait trop facile de perdre son chemin, de faire ce qu'ont fait les parents. Nous devons donc changer comme nous menons nos vies, si nous voulons devenir un pays sain.

2 Boulot et bac

This topic comes from the Learning and Employability areas, and allows you to talk about both school and a summer job. It will link into your future, allowing you to prepare an area for the conversation that follows on. Think about how you are going to structure your answer. Perhaps you might start off saying how you find studying and what your goals are. Then you could move on to talking about your job, saying where you are going to work. The next section could be about the clashes that sometimes occur for people doing part-time jobs, and you might finish off with the hope that it will all work out right in the end! Let's look at the first section, and remember not to go for lists in this area:

À présent je fais mes Highers, mon bac, afin de pouvoir aller plus tard à l'université, si je les réussis. Je fais cinq Highers, et il me faut faire deux heures de devoirs chaque soir, et même le weekend aussi ! Donc je n'ai pas de petit boulot, car je trouve que cela m'empêcherait de faire de mon mieux dans mes examens. Il m'est important d'avoir de bonnes notes pour arriver dans l'université de Glasgow.

This has given you the chance to put in some opinions, hope and reasons. In the next section you can try to move away from just *je*, and use the third person to give a better variety of structures. It also gives you the chance to vary your tenses:

La plupart des élèves dans ma classe ont quand même un petit boulot. Ils travaillent pour gagner de l'argent, car comme ça on peut se payer des vêtements ou sortir le weekend. Le boulot leur offre de l'indépendance de leurs parents : ils ne dépendent plus de leurs parents pour leur argent de poche. Moi, j'ai travaillé dans un supermarché deux soirs par semaine, pendant un mois, mais c'était trop pour moi.

This leads you into the clashes; again, try to generalise it by talking about others as well:

> Mes copains de classe et du travail ont quelquefois d'assez grands problèmes à combiner les devoirs et le boulot : souvent il arrive qu'on doive faire des heures supplémentaires le même jour que l'on a un devoir a rédiger pour le prof d'anglais. Si on refuse les heures supplémentaires, on risque de perdre son emploi, mais évidemment si on ne prépare pas ses devoirs, on risque la colère du prof, et de ne pas réussir ses examens.

Remember to keep putting in the little extra words, like *assez* and *évidemment*, which make your language flow better. Moving on to the last section, this is a chance to change tenses and introduce conditional and future, as well as a subjunctive if you feel comfortable with this:

> Naturellement je veux moi aussi gagner mon propre argent, donc je travaillerai cet été pendant six semaines dans un magasin, pour éviter des conflits entre les études et le travail. Mon espoir est que je continuerai à réussir, et je voudrais bien continuer de gagner de l'argent, mais je n'aimerais pas que mes notes souffrent endommagées par mon boulot, donc je ferai bien attention dans l'avenir, parce que pour moi le plus important sera de pouvoir aller en fac l'année prochaine.

3 Les voyages

This topic comes from the Culture context, and allows you to bring in a variety of tenses and structures, mentioning past visits and your future plans. You might start with a general statement about how you love travelling, and why, then move on to a mention of a journey you particularly liked or disliked, finishing up with your plans for next summer, mentioning who you are travelling with. The first section could look like this:

> J'habite une petite ville en Écosse, et je l'aime bien, mais quand même j'adore faire des voyages, surtout de longs voyages à l'étranger. ⇒

> J'aime voyager pour un tas de raisons, d'abord parce que j'aime les voyages eux-mêmes, être dans un train ou un avion. J'aime aussi rencontrer des gens que je ne connais pas, me faire de nouveaux amis. Finalement je l'aime, pouvoir parler une autre langue.

That section allowed you to put together a list of three reasons, but to introduce them with different words. You could also have used: *premièrement, deuxièmement, troisièmement*. These kinds of words help you remember what comes next. For the next section, let us look at two different ways of proceeding, both allowing you to introduce past tenses:

> Mais je me souviens d'un voyage qui était moins réussi. Je suis parti avec l'école pour passer une semaine dans les Alpes, et nous avons eu un tas de problèmes. Pour commencer, le bus était peu confortable, et tout le monde se sentait malade pendant le voyage, qui a en plus pris vingt-trois heures. Puis l'hôtel était très sale, et les repas étaient vraiment dégoûtants. Enfin les professeurs se sont fâchés, car quelques élèves ont bu de l'alcool. Mais, j'ai appris une chose importante : je ne repartirai jamais avec l'école.

Again, we have produced a list of reasons with different introductory words, to help learn the presentation. We have also shown we can use the two different past tenses correctly, and finished off with a future tense. We have also given reasons, and used complex sentences with conjunctions, which give the necessary structures for a good grade. Now let us look at the final part: most of the first two paragraphs were with *je*, although we also used the third person. So we should change this and use perhaps *nous*:

> Cette année, je veux partir avec mes parents en France : nous voulons aller au Midi, pour préciser à la Côte d'Azur. Nous irons à un camping, parce que comme ça c'est moins cher. Je sais qu'il y a des désavantages de voyager avec ses parents, mais nous nous entendons bien, et ce sera probablement la dernière fois que nous partirons ensemble, car l'année prochaine, mes copains et moi, on compte aller ensemble en Espagne après notre bac. Là, nous nous amuserons bien !

This final paragraph also allows you to lead the conversation that follows into areas such as advantages and disadvantages of travelling with parents and friends, and how you get on with your family and your friends. This way you can have a certain amount of control over what happens next.

The follow-up discussion

Remember the presentation is for you to control totally, and it should allow you to get started successfully, and settle your nerves. Next comes the discussion, which will start in the topic area you have used in the presentation, but will go beyond that. This is less predictable, but you can still retain a certain amount of control over what happens, and where the conversation goes. If you can give full answers to the questions, and also ask some questions of your own, then you should expect to answer something like twelve to fifteen questions in the time allocated. Shorter answers will inevitably lead to more questions, and are less likely to let you show off all the things that will get you good grades.

You can start the conversation off by leaving some good starting points in your presentation for where the conversation goes next. This makes it easy for the 'interlocutor', normally your teacher, to ask the first questions, and for you to have a chance to prepare your answers. So in the topic *Le tabagisme et les jeunes*, you left hanging the topics of drink and peer pressure. In *Boulot et bac*, you left open the subject of learning, but also of your future. In *Les voyages*, it was advantages and disadvantages of travelling with parents and friends, and how you get on with your family and your friends generally.

When preparing for the conversation, it is important that you allow yourself the opportunity to demonstrate exactly the same things you have in the presentation, namely the control of structures and vocabulary, a variety of tenses, a structure to the answer, opinions and reasons, and so on. The best way to do this is to make your answers longer, which has the added advantage that you will have to answer fewer questions. If you have been able to think of longer answers, it also means that some of your answers can be quite short; this is useful when you cannot think of an answer, or you are going down a road the teacher is taking you, but you do not want to go!

One useful approach is the **one-two-three** approach: this means every answer should have three parts. If you are asked for instance, '*Qu'est-ce que vous allez faire dans votre boulot?*', then your answer could go:

(1) Je vais travailler dans un supermarché qui s'appelle …

(2) Là, je travaillerai normalement à la caisse.

(3) C'est un travail assez bien payé.

This allows the next question to be one that asks you what you think of your job. Again, when giving your opinion, stick to the one-two-three approach:

> (1) Je trouve le travail dans le supermarché assez ennuyeux
>
> (2) parce que travailler à la caisse est très répétitive
>
> (3) mais mes copains travailleront là aussi, donc ça va tout de même.

This has given you the opportunity to give reasons and use conjunctions. You might also have prepared another answer; the answer to the question: 'Pendant combien de temps est-ce que vous avez travaillé là?' The one-two-three approach should make it easier to have longer answers, but it also makes it easier to remember your answers, as you can either count them off mentally or on your fingers as a memory aid. So, after having given one answer, you might think it a good chance to add another answer in here, and this is another way to help you control the conversation. Therefore, you could add this answer to the previous one, and it can still sound natural!

> (1) J'ai travaillé dans le supermarché pendant un mois.
>
> (2) J'ai commencé au mois de mai, après mes examens
>
> (3) parce que je voulais gagner de l'argent.

This answer also invites the question, 'What do you do with the money?', to which you would have prepared the answer in advance.

In the *Boulot et bac* topic, one of the obvious questions was, 'Qu'est-ce que vous voulez faire après votre bac?' You have a choice here, as you could talk about your immediate plans, such as going on holiday with your friends, which allows you to develop this topic area, or you could talk about your plans to work, go to university or take a year out. If you stick to the latter, when you have said everything you can think of about university, and so on, you can then add to an answer a sentence such as, '*Mais dans le futur immédiat, je veux partir en vacances avec mes copines cet été*'. This will lead the conversation on to this area, which you can have prepared.

Let us look at another one-two-three answer to the question about your future plans:

> (1) Je ne suis pas certain de ce que je ferai.
>
> (2) Ou je pourrais aller directement à l'université, si je réussis mes examens.
>
> (3) Ou je pourrai trouver un travail pour un an, les deux possibilités ont des avantages et des désavantages.

Sample paper

Let us look at an example of a Directed Writing paper. After this, we will look at the kind of general basic answers you should be prepared to write, which should help you write an essay based on this question. When you have done that, take it to your teacher and ask them (very nicely, of course!) to mark it.

Question ?

Scenario 1: Employability

You have recently returned from France, where you have been working.

On your return, you have been asked to write an account of your experiences to try to encourage other pupils to do the same thing.

You must include the following information and **you should try to add** other relevant details:

- What your job was **and** what you thought of it
- What you had to do in your job
- What you liked/disliked about the people you worked with
- If you would recommend such an experience to others

Question ?

Scenario 2: Culture

Last winter you went with a group of students from your school/college to a town in France for a few days. While you were there you went to a market.

On your return you were asked to write a report, **in French**, of your visit.

You must include the following information and **you should try to add** other relevant details:

- Where you went **and** what you thought of the accommodation
- What you did while you were there
- What you liked/disliked most about the experience
- How you plan to keep in touch with the friends you made there

Your first decision is which scenario to choose, and you should make this decision quickly. When you have done so, put a line through the other one, so you do not make a mistake and answer bits from both! The reason for your choice should be: which one do I have most points with answers already prepared?

You will see that there are four bullet points you have to cover, as well as bearing in mind the instructions in the box. This means you cannot simply prepare a piece of writing, learn it, and then write it out again in the exam. There are four possible contexts, but only two will be on offer in the exam.

Some of the bullet points are predictable, but others will be unique to that exam, so you will have to be ready to be flexible. You have to write 120 to 150 words in total, so a good rule of thumb is that each bullet point should have at least 30 words, with one or two being a bit longer. If your writing is unbalanced, you might lose points. This guideline also makes it easier to keep track of how much you are writing, rather than always recounting words and wasting time. It is really important to notice that the first bullet point has two parts, both parts of which you must answer, or you will lose marks.

Scenario 1

Let us look at the first scenario:

- *What your job was and what you thought of it*

For this, you know it was a summer job, so you can start off with a general introduction, then choose a job you have perhaps already done at home, as you will have the vocabulary for this. For part two, go for a positive and a negative viewpoint, to vary your structures and to allow you to use more pre-learned material:

Cette année, au mois de juin, je suis partie pour aller à Lille, dans le nord-est de la France. Là, j'ai travaillé dans un café comme serveuse. Les autres serveuses étaient très sympathiques, mais le patron était un peu sévère. Quand même je me suis bien amusée.

Opinions are always worth fitting in, as you can have the sentences ready, with just a word or two to alter. Note that this has been answered as a girl, so all the endings agree with that.

- *What you had to do in your job*

You can use simple points, but make them more complex by adding sub-clauses with opinions, which again you can have ready and just fit in. Do not use lists; just a couple of points with opinions:

J'ai dû servir les clients dans le café et sur la terrasse, ce qui était très bien, parce que je parlais beaucoup de français. De temps en temps je faisais la vaisselle dans la cuisine, mais je n'aimais pas ça, car il faisait très chaud là.

- *What you liked/disliked about the people you worked with*

You have already mentioned likes and dislikes, but go on to do something similar here:

Les autres serveuses étaient très sympathiques, mais le patron était un peu sévère. J'ai beaucoup appris dans son café, parce qu'il m'a montré comment servir les clients. Quand même je me suis bien amusée.

- *If you would recommend such an experience to others*

This is almost certainly going to come up, so be ready for this. Think future and conditional tenses, and have a set of phrases ready to use:

J'ai tellement apprécié ma visite que je recommanderais un tel emploi à tout élève écossais. C'était une visite très réussie. Je voudrais y retourner l'année prochaine, parce que, comme ça, je parlerai plus de français et je pourrai améliorer mon accent.

Scenario 2

Now have a look at the second scenario, and see how you can adapt the answer above to fit that.

- *Where you stayed and what you thought of the accommodation*

You can use the same first sentence, and vary the answer to fit the bullet point:

L'année dernière, au mois de décembre, je suis partie pour aller à Lille, dans le nord-est de la France. Là, je suis restée dans un hôtel avec les autres de ma classe. L'hôtel était très agréable, mais le patron était un peu sévère. Quand même je me suis bien amusée.

- *What you did while you were there*

Nous avons visité un café et tous les petits magasins, ce qui était très bien, parce que je parlais beaucoup de français. Nous avons acheté beaucoup de cadeaux pour nos familles, car il y avait des choses très différentes de chez nous.

- *What you liked/disliked most about the experience*

Le patron de l'hôtel était assez sévère, mais j'ai beaucoup aimé notre séjour, parce que l'hôtel était très propre. Je n'aimais pas beaucoup le temps, parce qu'il faisait assez froid, mais j'adorais parler avec tous les jeunes Français que j'ai rencontrés.

- *How you plan to keep in touch with your new friends in the future*

What new friends, you ask! The answer can be that you made new friends in your school group, or that you met someone in France. You might go for the last bit, because that is something you should have prepared, as you are very likely to be asked about how you got on with people in France in the actual exam. And remember: use the future and conditional:

J'ai fait de nouvelles amies françaises au marché de Noël, et je voudrais rester en contact avec elles. On va s'écrire, parce que nous nous sommes bien entendues et nous avons beaucoup rigolé. J'aimerais retourner en France cette été pour leur rendre visite.

Preparing for writing

What will you find easiest to prepare? Here is a list of things that are liable to come up:

☞ How you got there
(you can prepare this in advance, but be ready to change methods of transport and times or dates)
☞ What you thought of the people you were with
(have a positive and a negative sentence ready for this)
☞ What the journey was like
☞ Where you stayed and what you thought of it
(this could be the house, the hostel, the town or the area)
☞ What you did when you were there
(this is an area where you will have to have different ideas ready, as you may be on a work experience, school exchange, sports trip, school visit, family visit, and so on)
☞ What you thought of what you were doing
(have a positive and a negative opinion ready) ⇨

⇒
☞ *What you did in the evenings*
  (more predictable!)
☞ *What you thought of the place or people you stayed or*
  worked with
☞ *Whether you will do such a visit again, and why*
  (this makes you put in a future or conditional tense)
☞ *How you will keep in touch with people you met*

Let's look at some of these, one at a time.

How you got there

Neither of the scenarios exemplified above specifies this, but it counts as 'other relevant details', so it is worth having a sentence ready.

If we assume you went to France, you can choose your method of transport, unless the question actually specifies the method. You should also be able to put in when you went, as this is relevant. However, you might also have to change these details. This is liable to be the start to your writing, so start off well to impress the examiner:

> L'année dernière, au mois de juin, je suis parti pour aller à Lille, dans le nord-est de la France. Nous sommes allés en train.

This is quite straightforward, and would lead into most scenarios. We have also varied the subject and the structures, so that every sentence does not start off with *je*. Note, this is for a boy.

This part should be short, and would only go on if you were asked to describe the journey, as it could otherwise be seen as using irrelevant material. You must make sure your answers are relevant to the questions asked.

Where you stayed

This might be a family home, or hostel or other accommodation. If staying with a family, this can be very straightforward; just a simple description of the house and your room with of course, as usual, an opinion:

> Ma famille habitait une petite maison qui avait trois chambres, à deux kilomètres de l'école. Moi, j'avais une petite chambre pour moi, et j'en étais content, car chez moi je dois partager une chambre avec mon frère.

If you are in student accommodation, the answer can be very similar:

> J'étais logé dans un bâtiment à deux kilomètres de l'université. Moi, j'avais une petite chambre pour moi, et j'en étais content, car chez moi je dois partager une chambre avec mon frère.

What you did when you were there

This will depend very much on the scenario set at the top of the task, but still there will be common structures you can use throughout the different scenarios. There are two different areas here as well: the first is what you did during the day; the second is what you did in your leisure time.

Firstly let us look at what you could write about the daytime. This will depend very much on whether you are describing a visit to a school, family, and so on, or whether you are working. If you are visiting someone, then you will be able to use the following kind of language:

> Tous les jours on a fait des visites : on est allés par exemple au centre-ville de Lille pour voir les musées, et on a fait une visite en bus à une brasserie, où on a pu essayer de la bière française : c'était amusant de voir nos profs avec un verre à la main, et j'ai pris une photo pour faire chanter (blackmail) Mme Vernier !

If you are visiting a family, use this as an opportunity to use third-person verbs, as well as *nous* and *on*, as this gets away from always using *je*. Note that this answer is for a boy; for a girl, probably use *ma corres* or ma copine (mon copain) and *emmenée:*

> Les parents de mon corres m'ont emmené en Belgique, où on a pris un bateau-mouche à Bruges : c'était extra, car on a vu tous les canaux.

If you are attending a school, then you can describe the school, the teachers and what you thought of some of the lessons:

> Le lycée était très grand : il y avait 1800 élèves en tout dans un bâtiment immense, et tellement de professeurs que je ne reconnaissais personne. J'ai participé à des cours d'anglais (marrant) et de maths (épatant). On n'a pas pu faire du sport, ce qui était dommage.

If you are working, or taking part in work experience, then you can describe your job and what you thought of it. Note that this answer is for a girl:

> J'ai travaillé dans un hôtel comme serveuse, ce qui était assez difficile, car tout le monde parlait en français, bien sûr. Le travail était dur, mais j'ai reçu beaucoup de pourboires, donc j'étais très contente finalement.

What you did in the evenings

You are likely also to be asked to write what you did during your free time, in the evenings or at the weekends. The following answers are all for a male writer. This might be mixed up with what you did generally, but you can probably use this section whatever the topic. Here is one suggestion, but you should prepare your own and have it ready to use:

Je suis allé au cinéma une fois avec un groupe de copains : pour moi, c'était la première fois que j'ai vu un film en français sans sous-titres, et je n'en ai pas compris beaucoup.

What you thought of the place or people you stayed or worked with

You are very likely to be asked about your impressions of the other people there, or how you got on with them, or else what you thought of where you stayed. This is pretty predictable, with just a few changes necessary to meet the context. For instance, for your fellow students:

Je me suis très bien entendu avec les autres étudiants. Ils étaient tous sympa, et nous restons en contact par mail et par sms. Surtout j'ai aimé Vincent, qui a passé beaucoup de temps avec moi, et qui m'a aidé à parler français.

Or your host family:

Je me suis très bien entendu avec ma famille. Ils étaient tous sympa, et nous restons en contact par mail et par lettre. Surtout j'ai aimé la mère de mon corres, qui a passé beaucoup de temps avec moi, et qui m'a aidé à parler français.

Whether you will do such a visit again, and why/How you will keep in touch with people you met

Usually you will be asked as a final bullet point to use future and/or conditional tenses, by saying how you will keep in touch, whether you would do the visit again or how you will be helped in the future by your experience. This could be done by giving your plans for next year; saying when you will complete the exchange, or go back to the same place; describing how you will keep in touch; or by saying how much better your French is and what a confident mature person you have become! First of all, plans for the future:

> En septembre mon corres (copain) reviendra chez nous avec
> sa classe : ils vont passer dix jours chez notre école, ce qui sera
> fantastique ! Pour l'instant, on va s'écrire des mails chaque semaine,
> et bien sûr j'enverrai des SMS (messages texte) si j'aurai de l'argent
> dans mon phone ! L'année prochaine, je voudrais bien retourner
> là-bas tout seul pour passer l'été à travailler et à apprendre plus de
> français.

And now, boasting about how wonderful your French has become! Into this you have even managed to get a subjunctive – *bien que j'aie*:

> J'ai parlé beaucoup, et bien que j'aie fait pas mal d'erreurs, j'ai fait
> aussi fait du progrès sérieux. Cela m'aidera l'année prochaine, quand
> je compte aller à l'université pour faire des études de français.

Conclusion

So, hopefully you can see that the directed writing is not just a leap in the dark: most of the bullet points you can have well prepared, as long as you are able to be flexible. Now try to write your own answer for one of the scenarios in the sample paper on page 79, and show your work to your teacher.

What you should do next is look at the directed writing in other past or practice papers, which you can either buy or ask your teacher to show you. Look at the bullet points in each of them, and see how much of each of these papers you can prepare in advance. You should also look at the bullet points that present unexpected material, and plan how you would answer them.

Chapter 11
Personal response writing

Introduction

During your Higher exam, remember you will have to produce two pieces of writing, and that writing altogether makes up 20 per cent of your overall mark. The personal response writing is one of these two pieces, and is worth 10 marks. It is a piece of writing that is a personal response to the topic that is the focus of the Listening paper. This means you will not know in advance what the subject of the personal response is, and you will have about 40 minutes in the exam to plan and produce the final piece of writing.

However, this is not as bad as it sounds. Firstly, you will only have to write between 120 and 150 words. Secondly, the themes and topics of the exam you will have covered over the year of the Higher Course, so the topic should not be one that is new to you. And finally, as this is a personal response, which means you have to give your opinion, you can have a lot of your answer prepared in advance.

The contexts from which the listening is taken are quite clear; that is to say, the four contexts of Society, Learning, Employability and Culture. The exact topic will not be obscure, but rather one you would expect to cover in depth over the course of your Higher year, and you should make a point of collecting relevant phrases and sentences on the topics you cover to give you a bank of material to work from when preparing these tasks. It is also really common to be asked about the future, so make sure you have some future and conditional verbs and phrases prepared. You will find a full list of the contents and topics in Appendix 1.

Your writing will be marked according to how well it demonstrates a sense of structure, control of grammar, variety of vocabulary and also how relevant it is. The way of judging how well you have done is given in the criteria for personal writing: these are in Appendix 4, and will let you see what is expected of you if you are aiming for a specific mark. However, what lets many people down is that they do not answer properly the actual questions that are given in the Listening paper, but write out an essay they know quite well on a similar topic.

Remember
You should develop a range of good phrases that you can adapt to any topic.

Sample question

Once you know your topic area, focus on the actual language you will use. Look carefully at the overall topic, then the three leading questions, to make sure you answer them all in your response. Your personal response must address all of these, or you will lose marks. Here is a sample question from SQA, which comes from the context of Learning, but could also allow you to use some vocabulary from Employability:

Question

Audrey nous a parlé de son expérience au lycée et de ses projets d'avenir. Penses-tu comme Audrey que les langues sont importantes pour l'avenir? Est-ce que ton lycée/collège te prépare bien pour le monde du travail? As-tu des projets précis pour le futur?

Écris 120–150 mots en français pour exprimer tes idées.

You are asked to talk about what you think of the importance of languages for the future, which is quite straightforward, and should allow you to introduce material you will know well. Secondly, you are asked if your school is preparing you for the future. Finally, you are asked about your future plans. Ideally, you should plan to answer each of these questions in about 40 words. You could also have a start and a finish ready, which would mean you have good structure to your writing. The introduction could be just a rephrasing of the question.

So you might start off with something like this:

Je voudrais bien parler un peu de mes expériences à l'école, et aussi de mes projets d'avenir.

You know these words are correct, as you have just taken them from the paper, and they are the very first words you could apply to any topic. You might then carry on in response to the first question:

À mon avis, les langues étrangères sont très importantes pour nous en Écosse. J'apprends le français, bien sûr, parce que c'est nécessaire pour ce que je veux faire. Je fais aussi l'espagnol, parce que c'est une langue que l'on parle partout en Amérique.

This is about 40 words and, although it is very simple and straightforward, it does answer the question and also allows you to put in sub-clauses and adjectives, which show you can use structures.

The next question is about your school. Try to choose one aspect you are happy with, and one not; this allows you to give different opinions. Then you could continue:

Chapter 12

Structures and vocabulary

Introduction

For your Higher French, you will have to produce a variety of pieces of work in French. For Speaking, these are the presentation and discussion, and for Writing, the directed writing as well as the personal response, along with the work you produce for the Using Language Unit assessments. You will be assessed in both skills on, amongst other things, your use of structure, your ability to give opinions and reasons and the accurate use of a variety of grammatical structures and vocabulary. The SQA marking scheme mentions the following points relating to Language Resource for a top mark.

What you should know

★ The language used is detailed and complex.
★ There is good use of adjectives, adverbs, prepositional phrases and, where appropriate, word order.
★ A comprehensive range of verbs/verb forms, tenses and constructions is used.
★ Some modal verbs and infinitives may be used.
★ The candidate is comfortable with the first person of the verb and generally uses a different verb in each sentence.
★ Sentences are mainly complex and accurate.
★ The language flows well.

Structure

Structure means that your work should be directly related to the topic you are writing or speaking about. You will lose marks for work that is unorganised and irrelevant to the question set.

For your **presentation**, as well as for the **personal response**, structure also means introducing the topic, giving your information and your opinions and coming to a conclusion.

For the **directed writing**, structure means following the bullet points, and addressing each of the points adequately, as well as using some more complex language.

Giving opinions and reasons

Giving opinions is crucial to any personal response, and also to any presentation or follow-up discussion. It is worth mastering all the vocabulary you learned for National 5, so that it falls easily to you and you don't have to think about it. Make sure you have a variety of phrases, and do not just stick to your favourite three or four. To remind you, here is what you should know already:

J'aime, J'adore, Je préfère	*I like, love, prefer*
Je n'aime pas, Je déteste	*I don't like, I hate*
J'ai horreur de …	*I really hate …*
Je trouve que c'est …	*I think that it's …*
Je trouve cela formidable	*I find that terrific*
Je trouve bête que …	*I find it stupid that …*
C'est fantastique, très bien, génial	*It's fantastic, very good, great*
intéressant, passionnant, marrant	*interesting, exciting, fun*
C'est minable, triste, déprimant	*It's awful, sad, depressing*
pénible, nul, ennuyeux	*terrible, no good, boring*
Il est mieux/pire de …	*It is better/worse to …*
Il y a (Il y avait) trop de …	*There is/are (There was/were) too much/many …*
Il n' y a pas assez de …	*There is not enough …*
Il serait utile de pouvoir …	*It would be useful to be able to …*
À mon avis	*In my opinion*
Il faut penser à …	*You have to think about …*
Il ne faut pas oublier que …	*We mustn't forget that …*
Nous devons …/Nous ne devons pas …	*We should …/We shouldn't …*
J'aimerais savoir que …	*I would like to know that …*
Je voudrais voir …	*I would like to see …*

However, for Higher, you need to do more with these. You need to start giving reasons for your opinions. When answering a question in the discussion, on whether you are interested in sport, it is not enough to say:

Non, je n'aime pas le sport.

You have to build on this, and say something like:

Non, je n'aime pas le sport, car je le trouve bête qu'on doive sortir par la pluie pour participer à une activité que je ne supporte pas.

93

Conjunctions

This leads us on to the next part: conjunctions. Get into the habit of giving a reason when you give an opinion, and get into the habit of using conjunctions all the time. It will make your writing or speaking flow better, which means better structured work and a better mark.

Using conjunctions

Giving reasons for your opinions can be done by simply stating the reason. However, it is much better for your work to use a conjunction, as this allows you to use more complex grammatical structures. How many do you know? Start off with those below, and add more as you come across them, and start using them. Look at the sentences, and try to work out what they mean:

mais	but	J'aime bien le sport, mais je ne suis pas fanatique.
car	because	J'adore bien ma sœur, car je peux lui parler de tout.
parce que	because	Je le trouve nul, parce que c'est très difficile et m'embête.
comme	as	Je ne veux pas sortir, comme il pleut.
donc	so	Je la trouve minable, donc je préfère ne pas y aller.
par conséquent	therefore	J'ai trouvé la géo très difficile, par conséquent je n'en fais plus.
quand	when	Je voulais sortir, quand ma mère m'a persuadé de rester.
lorsque	when	Lorsque j'étais plus jeune, j'aimais Kylie, mais maintenant, je ne la supporte pas.
pendant que	while	Pendant que je serai en vacances, je voudrais rester en forme.
comment	how	Je ne comprends pas comment je peux faire plus d'effort.
si	if	Je me demande si je l'aime ou non.
ce que	what	Ce que je n'aime pas, c'est la violence dans la rue.

Grammatical structures

Your grade at Higher (and even your pass/fail) will depend upon your accuracy with grammatical structures. The grammar guide in Appendix 2 will give you an overview of what you should know, but below briefly are the main things you should be doing. If you do not understand any of them, then find out what they mean.

What you should know

- ★ Get the gender and plural form of your nouns right.
- ★ Attach adjectives to nouns with the correct endings and in the correct place.
- ★ Use comparatives.
- ★ Use a variety of negatives with your verbs.
- ★ Use pronouns correctly: that means the correct form, the correct gender and in the correct place.
- ★ Use reflexive pronouns (and reflexive verbs) correctly.
- ★ Use prepositions correctly.

And of course knowing about verbs is the single most important thing you can do! You need to get those endings right, which means learning them, but also knowing how to check them in a dictionary, as French has quite a few irregular verbs that do not follow the normal pattern. Here are the tenses you should know and understand: it is your job to match these up with the correct endings.

The present

The present tense only has one form, unlike in English. Make sure you do not try to translate 'I am working at home' word for word: this is *Je travaille à la maison.* Equally, 'When do you go?' does not need the word *fais* in French.

The past

You should be able to use at least three tenses in the past. These tenses have various names, although most books refer to them as the perfect, the pluperfect and the imperfect. You should use the perfect to talk about a single event in the past, and the imperfect to describe how things were, used to be, or how things were often:

Je suis parti à six heures du matin.

Il faisait mauvais.

Il faisait souvent mauvais cet hiver.

The pluperfect is used in complex sentences when one thing happened before the other:

I had already eaten when he arrived.

J'avais déjà mangé lorsqu'il est arrivé.

You might also come across a verb tense called 'the past historic' or *passé simple.* You do not, however, have to be able to use this for Higher, but some of the texts you read may feature it.

The future

You should be able to use the informal future, the formal future and the conditional:

On va visiter la France cet été.

J'irai avec mes copines.

J'aimerais aller à Paris.

You should also be able to recognise the subjunctive, and use it at some points in your writing. It may sound difficult, but a French toddler who needs to go to the toilet urgently will shout out '*Il faut que j'aille*': if a French two-year-old can use the subjunctive, so can you! You will find some examples of this in the chapter on talking (Chapter 9).

Vocabulary

The vocabulary you will need is the vocabulary you work on as you go through the Course, so make sure you keep a note of it in a way that makes sense to you. That might be in a vocabulary book, in spidergrams or in a folder divided into topics. However, included here are some adjectives and adverbs, as well as some basics that include numbers from earlier for you to revise from, as it will be assumed that you know them. It is amazing how many people get them wrong during the Listening assessments!

Adjectives

Adjectives are useful for giving opinions, and for improving the quality of your speaking and writing. Here are a few to work from, but add your own as you come across them. If you do not know them, look them up! And remember, if you want the best marks for talking and writing, you should attach these adjectives to nouns. Make sure they are in the correct place – normally after the noun – and that they agree, if necessary:

C'était une visite affreuse. Ma journée préférée était …

affreux	désagréable	nul	rigolo
agréable	embêtant	ouvert	sain
autoritaire	ennuyeux	parfait	sale
barbant	extraordinaire	pas mal	sensible
bizarre	gênant	passionnant	seul
cher, pas cher	génial	patient	sévère
choquant	impressionnant	pénible	strict
chouette	magnifique	pratique	sympa
cool	malade	préféré	vieux
démodé	modeste	raisonnable	

Adverbs

Adverbs describe and modify verbs, but they are also very useful with adjectives, to make your language seem more natural:

C'est absolument nul ! Je le trouve légèrement ennuyeux.

Get into the habit of using them. Here are a few to start with:

absolument	extrêmement	même	très
assez	fortement	un peu	trop
bien	jamais	totalement	
en général	légèrement	toujours	

Times

neuf heures	*nine o'clock*
neuf heures et quart	*quarter past nine*
neuf heures vingt	*twenty past nine*
neuf heures et demie	*half past nine*
neuf heures moins le quart	*quarter to nine*
neuf heures moins cinq	*five to nine*
midi et demi, minuit et demi	*half past tweve*

Remember most official times in French will use the 24-hour clock, and there is no use of a.m. and p.m.

treize heures	*one p.m.*
dix-huit heures trente	*6.30 p.m.*
le matin	*morning*
l'après-midi	*afternoon*
le soir	*evening*
la nuit	*night*

Seasons

le printemps	l'été	l'automne	l'hiver

⇨

être partagé entre	*to be torn between*
être sollicité	*to be in demand*
manifester contre	*to protest against*
manquer	*to miss*
se mettre à	*to get down to, to start*
se passer bien	*to go smoothly*
profiter de	*to take advantage of*
se rappeler	*to remember*
réclamer	*to ask for something*

Vocabulary for specific topic areas

Society: family members

la famille	*family*
les parents	*parents*
le père	*father*
la mère	*mother*
le mari	*husband*
la femme	*wife*
le frère, mon frère aîné/mon frère cadet	*brother, my older/my younger brother*
la sœur, ma sœur aînée/ma sœur cadette	*sister, my older/my younger sister*
le fils	*son*
la fille	*daughter*
un jumeau/une jumelle	*twin*
le grand-père	*grandfather*
la grand-mère	*grandmother*
un petit-fils/une petite-fille/les petits-enfants	*grandson/granddaughter/grandchildren*
un oncle	*uncle*
une tante	*aunt*
un cousin/une cousine	*cousin*
un neveu	*nephew*
une nièce	*niece*

Starter sentences

Nous sommes quatre dans ma famille.	*There are four of us.*
Je n'ai pas de frères/sœurs/Je suis enfant unique.	*I don't have any brothers/sisters.*
J'ai une sœur et deux frères.	*I have a sister and two brothers.*
Mon frère/ma sœur s'appelle …	*My brother/sister is called …*
Mes parents s'appellent …	*My parents are called …*
Mes parents sont séparés/divorcés.	*My parents are separated/divorced.*
Je m'entends bien avec mes parents.	*I get on well with my parents.*
Mes parents sont très sympa.	*My parents are very nice.*
Quelquefois, j'ai des discutes/disputes avec ma mère.	*I sometimes have discussions/arguments with my mum.*
Ma sœur est très gentille.	*My sister is very nice.*
Je peux discuter de mes problèmes avec …	*I can speak about my problems with …*
Je ne m'entends pas bien avec mon frère.	*I don't get on well with my brother.*
Mon frère m'énerve.	*My brother annoys me.*

Society: family

le mariage	*marriage*
le divorce	*divorce*
le consentement mutuel	*mutual consent*
un homme au foyer	*househusband*
une femme au foyer	*housewife*
un mari/époux	*husband*
une épouse/femme	*wife*
la cellule familiale	*the family unit*
le taux de divorce	*divorce rate*
l'éducation des enfants (f)	*raising of the children*
l'alliance (f)	*wedding ring*
la lune de miel	*honeymoon*
la bague des fiançailles	*engagement ring*
l'anniversaire de mariage (m)	*wedding anniversary*
la grossesse	*pregnancy*
l'amitié (m)	*friendship*

$\Rightarrow$

⇨

la relation	relationship
les fiançailles (f)	engagement
les beaux-parents (m)	in-laws
un casse-tête	major problem, a headache
grandir	to grow up
le planning familial	family planning
le comportement	behaviour
le foyer	the home
le concubinage	living together
la cohabitation	living together
le congé maternité	maternity leave
l'état civil (m)	marital status
le mariage civil	registry marriage
le PACS	contract between two people living together, civil partnership
la famille (monoparentale)	(single-parent) family
l'union libre (f)	living together
le conflit des générations	the generation gap

Society: impact of the digital age

connecté	logged on
le cyber commerce	e-commerce
l'écran (m)	screen
le fichier	file
un informaticien	IT technician
l'internaute (m/f)	internet user
le mail	email message
le moteur de recherche	search engine
la pièce jointe	attachment
le pirate	hacker
le réseau	network
le site Web	website
le site Web de réseau social	social networking site

⇨

le SMS	*text message*
les solutions informatiques (f)	*IT solutions*
le soutien	*support*
TIC: Techniques de l'Information et de la Communication (f)	*ICT: Information and Communication Technologies*
le virus	*computer virus*

Society problems: drugs/alcohol/smoking

le tabagisme	*addiction to smoking*
le tabagisme passif	*passive smoking*
le SIDA	*AIDS*
le préservatif	*condom*
le toxicomane	*drug addict*
le trafiquant	*drug dealer*
le cancer du poumon	*lung cancer*
le centre de réadaption	*rehabilitation centre*
le cerveau	*brain*
la cirrhose du foie	*cirrhosis of the liver*
la conduite en état d'ivresse	*drink-driving*
les dommages irréversibles (m)	*irreversible damage*
les drogues dures (f)	*hard drugs*
les drogues douces (f)	*soft drugs*
le foie	*liver*
la guérison	*cure*
la gueule de bois	*hangover*
l'héroïnomane (m/f)	*heroin addict*
l'interdiction (f)	*ban*
l'ivresse (f)	*drunkenness*
le manque	*withdrawal symptoms*
la poussée de stupéfiants	*drug-pushing*
les problèmes respiratoires (m)	*breathing problems*
les retombées (f)	*side-effects*
le sevrage	*weaning off drugs*

⇒

le stupéfiant	*drug*
la toxicomanie (f)	*drug addiction*
la toux du fumeur	*smoker's cough*
la volonté	*will power*
avoir/former une dépendance à	*to be/become addicted to*
boire à l'excès	*to drink to excess*
se droguer	*to take drugs*
empêcher	*to prevent*
fumer	*to smoke*
nuire à	*to harm*

Learning: school subjects

l'allemand (m)	*German*
l'anglais (m)	*English*
la biologie	*biology*
la chimie	*chemistry*
le commerce	*business management*
le dessin	*art*
l'EMT (f)	*craft and design*
l'EPS (f)	*PE*
l'espagnol (m)	*Spanish*
le français	*French*
la géographie	*geography*
l'histoire (f)	*history*
l'informatique (f)	*IT*
les maths (m)	*maths*
la musique	*music*
la politique/l'instruction civique (f)	*modern studies*
la physique	*physics*
les sciences nat (f)	*science*
le sport	*sport*
la technologie	*technological studies*

School (general)

le collège/CES	*secondary school (S1–4)*
le lycée	*secondary school (S5/6)*
le bac/baccalauréat	*equivalent to Highers*
la bibliothèque	*library*
le bulletin	*report*
la cantine	*canteen*
le cours	*lesson*
les devoirs (m)	*homework*
l'élève (m/f)	*pupil*
les études (f)	*study, schoolwork*
l'examen (m)	*exam*
la fac/l'université (f)	*uni/university*
le laboratoire	*laboratory*
la matière	*a subject*
la pause de midi	*lunchtime*
le/la professeur	*teacher*
la récréation/récré	*morning interval, break*
la salle de classe	*classroom*
les vacances (f)	*holidays*
les grandes vacances (f)	*summer holidays*
les vacances de Pâques, de Noël (f)	*Easter, Christmas holidays*

Remember that French pupils would refer to fifth year as seconde *and use* terminale *for the last year in school. The equivalent of Highers would be the* bac.

Starter sentences

Je vais passer mes examens en mai.	*I'm going to sit my exams in May.*
J'espère réussir à mes examens.	*I hope to pass my exams.*
J'ai reçu de bonnes notes en …	*I got good marks in …*
Ma matière préférée est le français.	*My favourite subject is French.*
Ce que je n'aime pas du tout, c'est …	*What I really don't like is*
Je pense que le prof est moche.	*I think that the teacher is awful.*

⇨

Employability, general

l'artisanat (m)	*Arts and Crafts*
le chef d'entreprise	*company manager*
l'expatrié (m)	*expat*
gérer	*to manage*
l'intérim, intérimaire (m/f)	*temp, temporary worker*
le métier	*profession*
le monde de l'entreprise	*the business world*

Culture, travel: methods of transport

en auto/voiture	*by car*
en autobus/car	*by bus*
en avion	*by plane*
en bateau	*by boat*
en métro	*by underground*
à moto	*by motorbike*
à pied	*on foot*
en train	*by train*
à vélo	*by bike*

Starter sentences

Je vais au collège à pied, normalement.	*Usually I walk to school.*
Nous sommes allés en bus.	*We went by bus.*
Quand il pleut, je prends le bus.	*I go by bus when it's raining.*
Je préfère aller en voiture, c'est plus vite.	*I prefer going by car, it's quicker.*
Nous sommes allés en France en train.	*We went to France by train.*
Je préfère aller à vélo, c'est plus facile.	*I prefer to go by bike, it's easier.*

Culture: travel

l'auberge de jeunesse (f)	*youth hostel*
le bord de la mer	*seaside*
le centre touristique	*tourist resort*
le circuit touristique	*tourist circuit*
la colonie (le club) de vacances	*holiday camp*
le coût de la vie	*cost of living*
la croisière	*cruise*
le dépaysement	*change of scenery*
la détente	*relaxation*
les distractions (f)	*things to do*
l'emploi saisonnier (m)	*seasonal job*
l'estivant (m)	*holiday maker*
l'évasion (f)	*escape*
la haute saison	*high season*
l'hébergement (m)	*accommodation*
le littoral	*seashore*
la pension	*guest house*
la résidence secondaire	*holiday home*
le retour à la nature	*return to nature*
la station balnéaire	*seaside resort*
le tourisme	*tourism*
le tourisme rural	*cottage holidays*
le vacancier	*holiday maker*
la vie nocturne	*night life*
les vacances en location (f)	*self-catering holidays*
le voyage	*trip*
partir en vacances	*to go on holiday*
se détendre	*to relax*
abîmer	*to spoil*
apporter	*to bring*
approfondir votre connaissance du monde	*to deepen one's knowledge of the world*
élargir ses horizons	*to broaden one's horizons*
ouvrir l'esprit	*to open the mind*

Culture: media

à la une	*on the front page*
la bande dessinée, BD	*comic, also often a graphic novel*
le courrier du cœur	*agony aunt column*
la critique	*review*
le dessin animé	*cartoon*
la diffusion	*broadcast*
le divertissement	*entertainment*
le dossier	*issue, area of concern*
l'éditeur (m)	*publisher*
l'émission (f)	*programme*
l'émission d'actualité (f)	*news programme*
l'exemplaire (m)	*copy*
les faits divers (m)	*news in brief*
le feuilleton	*TV series, soap*
les gros titres (m)	*headlines*
les hebdomadaires (m)	*weekly newspapers*
les infos (f)	*news*
le journal	*newspaper*
le journaliste	*journalist*
la libre parole	*free speech*
la liberté de la presse	*freedom of the press*
le magasin de journaux	*newsagent's*
le magazine d'information	*news programme*
les médias (m)	*media*
les petites annonces (f)	*classified ads*
la presse de sensation	*tabloid press*
la publicité	*advertising*
la question d'actualité	*topical issue*
le quotidien	*a daily*
le quotidien populaire/un tabloïde	*tabloid*
le rédacteur	*editor*

⇨

⇨

le reportage sportif	*sports programme*
la revue d'actualité	*news magazine*
la rubrique (sportive)	*(sports) section/column*
les ventes (f)	*sales*
la vie privée	*private life*

Appendix 1

Contexts and topics of Higher French

Society	Family and friends	Becoming an adult/new family structure/marriage/partnership/gang culture/ bullying/social influences and pressures
	Lifestyle	Teenage problems, e.g. smoking, drugs, alcohol
	Media	Impact of the digital age
	Global languages	Minority languages and their importance/association with culture
	Citizenship	Global citizenship/democracy/politics/power
Learning	Learning in context	Understanding self as a learner, e.g. learning styles/importance of language learning
	Education	Advantages/disadvantages of higher or further education, choosing a university/college, lifelong learning
Employability	Jobs	Getting a summer job, planning for future jobs/higher education, gap year, career path, equality in the workplace
	Work and CVs	Preparing for a job interview/importance of language in global contexts, job opportunities
Culture	Planning a trip	Taking a gap year/working abroad (mobility)/travel
	Other countries	Living in a multicultural society/stereotypes/ prejudice and racism
	Celebrating a special event	Social influences on/importance of traditions, customs and beliefs in another country
	Literature of another country	Literature – analysis and evaluation
	Film and television	Studying the media of another country

Grammar guide: talking and writing

Grammar	Judging evidence at Higher The candidate:
Word order	• has control of different linguistic conventions in straightforward expressions and most more complex structures, e.g. noun/adjective order, relative and subordinate clauses • shows awareness of different linguistic conventions, e.g. noun/adjective order
Person	• uses subject and object pronouns consistently and shows awareness of the use of indirect object pronouns • uses reflexive and relative pronouns with common verbs in appropriate tenses
Tense and mood	• uses a range of tenses as appropriate, in particular present, future, perfect, imperfect, pluperfect, conditional • can ask a range of questions in different ways and can articulate commands • can use modal verbs plus infinitive in a range of tenses as appropriate • can use less common irregular verbs
Articles	• uses articles/determiners consistently and accurately
Cases and agreement	• shows some control of cases as appropriate in the language • uses correct adjective agreements with wide range of nouns (regular and irregular) • can use less common comparatives and superlatives
Prepositions	• can use common and less common prepositions and shows awareness of prepositional effects
Gender	• shows awareness of noun genders • uses correct adjective agreement with a wider range of nouns (regular and some irregular forms)

Content	Accuracy	Language Resource	Pegged Marks	
			Presentation	Conversation
<ul><li>Content is very basic, irrelevant and disorganised</li><li>Does not understand what is said</li><li>Hesitation and/or other language interference seriously impede communication</li></ul>	<ul><li>Virtually nothing is correct.</li><li>Very little, if anything, would be understood by a sympathetic speaker of the language.</li></ul>	<ul><li>There is no evidence of detailed and complex language.</li><li>There may be several examples of mother tongue interference.</li><li>English words are frequently used.</li></ul>	0	0

Conversation only – sustaining performance

5	3	0
Can sustain the conversation, responding to most questions and employing a range of techniques.	Can, with some help and prompting, adequately sustain the conversation and respond to some questions.	Unable to sustain the conversation and cannot go beyond the use of learned material.

Appendix 4

Marking instructions for directed and personal response writing

For the personal response writing, you are expected to address three aspects of the topic, put as three questions. If you do not address one of these aspects properly, your mark will move down a grade.

For the directed writing, you are expected to address **all four** bullet points, including **both** parts of the first bullet point.

i) If you fail to address one of the bullet points, the maximum mark that can be awarded is 6.

ii) If you fail to address two of the bullet points, the maximum mark that can be awarded is 4.

iii) If you fail to address three or more of the bullet points, the maximum mark that can be awarded is 0.

Mark	Content	Accuracy	Language Resource: variety, range, structures
10	<ul><li>The content is comprehensive.</li><li>The topic is addressed fully, in a balanced way.</li><li>Some candidates may also provide additional information.</li><li>Overall this comes over as a competent, well thought-out response to the task which reads naturally.</li></ul>	<ul><li>The language is accurate throughout. However, where the candidate attempts to go beyond the range of the task, a slightly higher number of inaccuracies need not detract from the overall very good impression.</li><li>A comprehensive range of verbs is used accurately and tenses are consistent and accurate.</li><li>There is evidence of confident handling of all aspects of grammar and spelling accurately, although the language may contain a number of minor errors, or even one serious major error.</li></ul>	<ul><li>The language used is detailed and complex.</li><li>There is good use of adjectives, adverbs, prepositional phrases and, where appropriate, word order.</li><li>A comprehensive range of verbs/verb forms, tenses and constructions is used.</li><li>Some modal verbs and infinitives may be used.</li><li>The candidate is comfortable with the first person of the verb and generally uses a different verb in each sentence.</li><li>The candidate uses co-ordinating conjunctions and subordinate clauses throughout the writing.</li><li>Sentences are mainly complex and accurate.</li><li>The language flows well.</li></ul>

Mark	Content	Accuracy	Language Resource: variety, range, structures
8	• The content is clear. • The topic is addressed clearly.	• The language is mostly accurate. However, where the candidate attempts to use detailed and complex language, this may be less successful, although basic structures are used accurately. • A range of verbs is used accurately and tenses are generally consistent and accurate. • There may be a few errors in spelling, adjective endings and, where relevant, case endings. Use of accents is less secure. • Verbs and other parts of speech are used accurately but simply.	• The language used is detailed and complex. • The candidate uses a range of verbs/verb forms and other constructions. • There may be less variety in the verbs used. • The candidate is comfortable with the first person of the verb and generally uses a different verb in each sentence. Most of the more complex sentences use co-ordinating conjunctions, and there may also be examples of subordinating conjunctions where appropriate. Sentences are generally complex and mainly accurate. • At times the language may be more basic than might otherwise be expected at this level. • There may be an example of minor misuse of dictionary. • Overall the writing will be very competent, essentially correct, but may be pedestrian.
6	• The content is adequate and may be similar to that of an 8 or a 10. • The topic is addressed adequately.	• The language may be mostly accurate. However, in places, control of the language structure may deteriorate significantly. • The verbs are generally correct, but basic. Tenses may be inconsistent, with present tenses being used at times instead of past tenses. • There may be errors in spelling, e.g. reversal of vowel combinations, adjective endings and some prepositions may be inaccurate or omitted, e.g. I went the town. There are quite a few errors in other parts of speech – personal pronouns, gender of nouns, adjective endings, cases, singular/plural confusion – and in the use of accents. • Overall, there is more correct than incorrect and there is the impression that the candidate can handle tenses.	• There are some examples of detailed and complex language. • The language is perhaps repetitive and uses a limited range of verbs and fixed phrases not appropriate to this level. The candidate relies on a limited range of vocabulary and structures. • There is minimal use of adjectives, probably mainly after 'is'. • The candidate copes with the present tense of most verbs. • Where the candidate attempts constructions with modal verbs, these are not always successful. • Sentences are mainly single clause and may be brief. • There may be some misuse of dictionary.

Mark	Content	Accuracy	Language Resource: variety, range, structures
4	• The content may be limited and may be presented as a single paragraph. • The topic is addressed in a limited way.	• The language used to address the more predictable aspects of the task may be accurate. However, major errors occur when the candidate attempts to address a less predictable aspect. • A limited range of verbs is used. • Ability to form tenses is inconsistent. • In the use of the perfect tense the auxiliary verb is omitted on a number of occasions. • There may be confusion between the singular and plural form of verbs. • There are errors in many other parts of speech – gender of nouns, cases, singular/plural confusion – and in spelling and, where appropriate, word order. • Several errors are serious, perhaps showing mother tongue interference. • Overall there is more incorrect than correct.	• There is limited use of detailed and complex language and the language is mainly simple and predictable. • The language is repetitive, with undue reliance on fixed phrases and a limited range of common basic verbs such as: to be, to have, to play, to watch. • There is inconsistency in the use of various expressions, especially verbs. • Sentences are basic and there may be one sentence that is not intelligible to a sympathetic native speaker. • An English word may appear in the writing or a word may be omitted. • There may be an example of serious dictionary misuse.
2	• The content may be basic or similar to that of a 4 or even a 6. • The topic is thinly addressed.	• The language is almost completely inaccurate throughout the writing and there is little control of language structure. • Many of the verbs are incorrect or even omitted. There is little evidence of tense control. • There are many errors in other parts of speech — personal pronouns, gender of nouns, cases, singular/plural confusion. • Prepositions are not used correctly.	• There is little, if any, use of detailed and complex language. • The candidate has a very limited vocabulary. • Verbs used more than once may be written differently on each occasion. • The candidate cannot cope with more than one or two basic verbs. • Sentences are very short and some sentences may not be understood by a sympathetic native speaker. • Several English or 'made-up' words may appear in the writing. • There are examples of serious dictionary misuse.
0	• The content is very basic. • The candidate is unable to address the topic.	• The language is seriously inaccurate throughout the writing and there is almost no control of language structure. • (Virtually) nothing is correct. • Most of the errors are serious. • Very little is intelligible to a sympathetic native speaker.	• There is no evidence of detailed and complex language. • The candidate copes only with 'have' and 'am'. • There may be several examples of mother tongue interference. • Very few words are written correctly in the modern language. • English words are used. • There may be several examples of serious dictionary misuse.